Beginner's
RUSSIAN

Beginner's
RUSSIAN

Nonna H. Carr &
Ludmila V. Rodionova
OF
EUROLINGUA

HIPPOCRENE BOOKS
New York

For information, address:
HIPPOCRENE BOOKS, INC.
171 Madison Avenue
New York, NY 10016

ISBN 0-7818-0232-6

Printed in the United States of America.

TABLE OF CONTENTS

Introduction 2

Geography 4

History 6

Political and Economic Situation 9

Culture and Art 11

Everyday Life 17

Language Lessons 27

Pronunciation Guide 28

Lesson One: Meeting people/Introduction 31

Lesson Two: Arrival at Moscow/Customs 39

Lesson Three: Taxi 45

Lesson Four: Hotel 51

Lesson Five: Post Office/Asking for Directions 57

Lesson Six: In the Restaurant 63

Lesson Seven: Shopping 73

Lesson Eight: Being a Guest 82

Lesson Nine: Illness 90

Lesson Ten: Socializing 98

Key to the Exercises 108

Review Exercise 111

Vocabulary 113

Russian-English Expressions 125

English-Russian Expressions 129

INTRODUCTION

The rich culture and languages of Eastern Europe are unique, intricate and subtle, steeped in tradition by hundreds of years of history. But, since the Eastern European countries were closed societies for over 40 years under communist rule, little is known about them.

After the fall of the Iron Curtain a flurry of activity is being spurred throughout Eastern Europe by the desire to establish democratic institutions and free market economies. Firms from the west are exploring business opportunities and expansion into these virtually untapped markets. A fresh and beautiful land together with the rich and exciting cultural heritage of its people has opened up for tourists to explore.

As a result, EUROLINGUA was started in September, 1990, to meet the growing demand for Eastern European languages and cross-cultural instruction. EUROLINGUA primarily serves tourists and business people who deal in international trade.

The passionate traveler would like to understand and enjoy the people and the customs of the country he will visit. For a successful international transaction the businessman has to know the appropriate conduct in various business situations. Finally, basic information about geography, history and politics of the country to be visited, together with some language knowledge will make anyone feel more at home.

These considerations have brought about this book, in the hope that it will become your friend and guide during your trip. The knowledge of customs, manners and some basics of language will help you discover more exiting things and make more friends than you have ever dreamed.

The book has two parts. The first part gives you information about the country (geography, history, economy, culture, customs and manners) and the second part consists of language lessons.

The language lessons are designed for the traveler and the nonspecialist amateur. You will learn useful phrases and words for special situations and basic grammar hints. The lessons will not cover all grammatical problems, nor will they give a rich vocabulary for sophisticated conversation. Instead they will teach you enough to feel comfortable in a variety of situations, which you will find described here.

With this small, compact book you will have in your pocket a collection of bits of information, sufficient to carry out satisfying interaction with the people of the country you visit, in their own language. It is the result of many hours of work, research and travel done by enthusiastic teachers and travelers who wish you good luck in your study and a wonderful trip.

4

GEOGRAPHY

Russia, or the Russian Federation, is the world's largest country with a total area of 17,075,400 square kilometers, or 6,592,846 square miles. It stretches from the Baltic Sea in the west to the Pacific Ocean in the east, and from the Arctic Ocean in the north to the Black Sea and Amur River in the south. Located both in Europe and Asia it is naturally divided by the Ural Mountains (with an average elevation of 488 meters, or 1,600 feet) into two parts: European Russia and Asian Russia, or Siberia. Because of different geographical features, Siberia, in turn, is divided into Western Siberia and Eastern Siberia. European Russia and Western Siberia are mainly plains, with altitudes not exceeding 460 meters (1,500 feet) above sea level, while Eastern Siberia consists of various mountains and plateau areas. Russia is so vast that it encompasses eleven time zones. By comparison, the Continental United States covers four.

The major rivers of Russia are among the largest in the world. The major river of European Russia is the Volga (the longest river in Europe). The major rivers in Siberia are the Ob, the Irtysh, the Yenisei, and the Amur, that flows along the Manchurian border. One of the most notable geographical features of Siberia is Lake Baikal, the world's deepest lake which is inhabited by many unique species of fish.

The climate of Russia is almost entirely of the continental type. It is characterized by a significant seasonal range of temperature that increases markedly from west to east. In the central European part of Russia the average temperature is approximately 70°F in summer and 10°F in winter. It is much colder in Siberia, where winter temperatures almost every year are reported as the lowest in the world. Because of the immense size of the country and the wide range of environmental conditions, flora and fauna of Russia offer a great deal of variety.

Moscow, the capital of the Russian Federation, is situated in the European part of Russia. It was founded in 1147 and since that time has become one of the largest cities in the world. Moscow is the center of the cultural, economic and political life of Russia.

The population of the Russian Federation is 149,527,479. It has density of 22.8 inhabitants per square mile (8.8 per square kilometer). The population of the capital is 9,000,000. There are many cities in Russia with a population of more than 1,000,000. The Russian Federation is a multi-ethnic country that includes 21 autonomous republics and regions. Approximately 81.5% of its population is Russian, 2.9% is Ukrainian, 0.8% is Byelorussian, 3.8% is Tatar, 1.2% is Chuvash. Ethnic Siberian people are the Yakuts, the Tuvinians, the Khakass, and the Altai. The Finno-Ugric group includes the Mordvinians, the Udmurts, the Mari, the Komi, and the Karelians. There are also other ethnic groups, such as the Germans, the Jews, the Bashkirs, etc.

HISTORY

The history of the Russian state began in about 1000 B. C. with the Cimmerians, who were overthrown by the Scythians around 700 B.C. The Scythians in turn yielded to a new group of Asian nomads, and these were followed by the Goths, the Huns, then the Avars and the Khasars.

The Slavs, who settled in this territory in approximately the 6th century, probably came from Poland and the Baltic shore.   These Eastern Slavs became the enduring Russians, the name they received in about the 9th century. The Slavs engaged in agriculture, hunting, fishing, and honey picking.

In 988 Russian Duke Vladimir I adopted Christianity from Greece and all the inhabitants of Kiev were baptized. After that, Kiev became the major cultural center, with many beautiful churches and monasteries in the Byzantine style. Kievan Rus prospered for about three centuries, dominating the main trade route from Scandinavia to Constantinople.

In the 13th century much of Europe and Asia was conquered by the Mongols. Kiev was sacked in 1240 by the khans of the Golden Horde, who established their control of Russia for about two centuries. Kiev was never to regain its political supremacy.   The devastation of southern Russia stimulated the growth of the north, of the trading center in Novgorod, and of the nearby town of Moscow. Moscovite Duke Dimitry Donskoi won the first great victory over the Mongols at Kulikovo in 1380.

After that victory and gaining power over other Russian towns, the main political aim of the grand dukes was to absorb the formerly independent principalities. "The gathering of the Russian land" was accomplished by Ivan IV (the Terrible, 1533-84). He assumed the title of tsar, conquered the khanates of Kazan (1552) and Astrakhan (1556), putting all territories along the Volga under the control of Russia. These conquests stimulated the expansion into Siberia (1581).

The death of tsar Ivan the Terrible began a generation of chaos, called the Time of Troubles, that was marked by dynastic struggles, social upheaval, and foreign intervention.

In 1613 the crown of Russia was offered to Mikhail Romanov, who established a dynasty that was to rule the country until 1917.

The next important stage of Russian history began in the 18th century under the rule of Peter I (the Great, 1682-1725). His reforms made Russia one of the great European nations. Victories in the wars with Sweden, Ottoman Turkey and Persia changed Russia's international position. Peter the Great "opened a window to Europe" for Russia by capturing the territories along the Baltic shore. In 1703 the building of the new capital, Saint Petersburg, began.

The main feature of the 18th century was the westernization of Russian culture. New educational institutions were opened in Russia (the Academy of Sciences, 1725; the University of Moscow, 1755). Many nobles traveled to Europe. Cultural westernization was accompanied by modernization of the Russian economy.

In 1812 Russia won the war with Napoleon I. But Russian peasants remained serfs. Serfdom slowed economic development of the country. The weakness of the Russian economic system became clear during the Crimean War (1853-56), which was disastrous for Russia. Russian society demanded new reforms, and in 1861 Alexander II abolished serfdom. After that Russia was set on the capitalist form of development.

In the beginning of the 20th century Russia moved toward scientific and cultural progress. Many scientific discoveries, an outburst of the arts, and a renaissance of religious life in Russia had a strong influence on the development of world culture. On the other hand, the years 1905-14 were a period of great political strain and confrontation. World War I strengthened contradictions in the Russian society and led to the overthrow of the tsarist regime and establishment of Communist power after the revolution in 1917.

During the Soviet period, Russia became a socialist industrial country. Lenin was the first leader of the communist government. Under the rule of Joseph Stalin, the USSR was isolated from the rest of the world, and more then 20,000 people were killed in concentration camps. Russia won a costly victory in World War II, but after that Stalin proclaimed a policy of "the iron curtain," which eliminated contacts with western democracies. Stalin's successor, Khrushchev criticized bloody repressions and Stalinism. For a short period Russia became more open toward the West and achieved great successes in science and technology. The first artificial space satellite was launched by Russia in 1957.

The era of the Cold War continued after Khrushchev was overthrown and replaced by Brezhnev until the beginning of Gorbachev's reforms in the late 1980s.

Gorbachev began removing the Communist party from its dominating position, but he was strongly against the separation of the republics from the Soviet Union. In August 1991 the coup of former party leaders who desired to restore the old order failed.

Soon the main role in the political life of Russia was passed to Yeltsin, the Russian president. In December 1991 the Soviet Union collapsed and Russia became an independent state.

POLITICAL AND ECONOMIC SITUATION

There have been great changes in Russia during the past few years. After the collapse of the USSR, the Russian government embarked on a program of radical economic reforms. The main aim was to establish a free market, to open the economy up to competition and private ownership. At the same time Russian politicians faced three tremendous tasks: building a constitutional state, leading society out of economic crisis, and re-defining Russia's role in the world.

Gorbachev's policy was unpopular and unproductive. Budget deficits and a very rapid increase of money supply led to inflation. Gorbachev tried to sustain the centralized socialist economy, which produced more economic problems. Boris Yeltsin began with privatization of small enterprises and state owned companies. Many shops, restaurants, small factories and enterprises have become private businesses, and the government has begun selling large plants through auctions. But Yeltsin faces enormous difficulties in privatization, not only of economic, but also of political character. One problem is increasing unemployment, the other is USSR's hard-currency debts. The political problem is the struggle of the President and his government against conservative parliament and the pro-communist Congress of the People's Deputies. The opposition accused the President of creating a disastrous situation for the majority of the population in Russia, who lost all their savings as a result of liberalization of prices, increasing inflation, and unemployment. The confrontation between legislative and executive branches reached its peak in the beginning of 1993, when Yeltsin decided to call for a referendum and ask people for support. This referendum was held on April 25, 1993. It showed that the majority of voters supported the President and his reforms. Yeltsin was promised strong financial help from the USA and other countries. But the referendum did not solve all the political problems. Yeltsin proclaimed the necessity of the adopting a new Constitution of the Russian Federation (the current Constitution was of the USSR and was adopted by the Communist Congress of the People's Deputies). According to the new Constitution, Russia will be the Presidential Republic with a new two-chamber Parliament. In spite of the continuing struggle between opposite parties in Russia, it is now clear that democratization and modernization of all spheres of social, economic, and political life are the only possibilities to lead the country out of the deepest crisis.

CULTURE AND ART

The Russian culture has great ancient traditions. The old Russian folk songs, architecture of the first Orthodox Christian churches, beautiful crafts, and colorful icons have become well known all over the world. The famous Russian writers of the 19th and 20th centuries: Pushkin, Dostoevsky, Tolstoi, Chekhov, Pasternak and Solzhenitsyn; remarkable composers: Glinka, Tchaikovsky, Rakhmaninov, Stravinsky; prominent painters: Repin, Perov, Vasnetsov, Levitan, Kandinsky, Malevich, all made great contributions to world culture.

Literature

The history of Russian literature began in the late 10th century, when Christianity was adopted by the Kievan Dukes. At first, it was closely connected to folklore. Most of the great ancient masterpieces were written in the old church Slavonic language.

In the 17th century and again during the era of Peter I, Russian literature became less dependent on the church and came more under the influence of European culture. Writers of the late 18th century were struggling for the modernization of national language.

At the beginning of the 19th century, the greatest Russian literary genius, Alexander Pushkin, completed the process of adapting the language as a literary vehicle. Pushkin started the new realistic trend in Russian literature. His famous novels "Eugene Onegin" and "Captain's Daughter" influenced the development of Russian literature in the 19th century.

Pushkin's traditions were continued by the greatest writers of the late 19th century: Turgenev, Dostoevsky and Tolstoi. The novel of Dostoevsky, "Crime and Punishment," depicted the struggle between rational (evil) and intuitive (kind) impressions of the world perceived by the human soul. The greatest masterpiece of Tolstoi, "War and Peace", raised humanitarian, philosophic and historic dilemmas. Later in the 1890s, the world-famous story writer Chekhov became a creator of the modern Russian drama, as well.

In the mid-1890s, inspired by European art, the new avant-garde movement began. One of them, symbolism, was the most influential. The most prominent authors of this movement were Blok, Briusov, and Bely. Later, symbolism was overlapped by futurism and acmeism. Mayakovsky, Akhmatova, and Gumilev participated in this group. At the same time one of the most original poet of his age, Boris Pasternak, began creating his poetry.

After the October Revolution of 1917 and continuing through the Stalinist era, literature came under political control of the communists. The main literary movement became "socialist realism." All writers were organized into one association, the Union of Writers of the USSR, with Maxim Gorky as the head of this Union. Even under severe suppression, the best writers, Bulgakov, Pasternak and Akhmatova, created their masterpieces that received worldwide recognition.

During Khrushchev's period, literary control was less pervasive, and publication of Solzhenitsin's novels became possible. During the 1960s a group of young progressive poets, including Yevtushenko and Voznesensky, wrote poems criticizing the Soviet regime.

Many talented artists emigrated from the country during the years of economic stagnation and suppression, which occurred during Brezhnev's rule. Brodsky, the most distinguished of the recent poets, Aksyonov, the famous novelist, and others were among them. Many talented authors continued to create their novels, short stories, and poems.

A new period began after 1985, when the policy of glasnost was proclaimed. The most famous contemporary Russian writers are Trifonov, Rasputin, Abramov, and Tolstaya.

Music

Russian music has achieved tremendous popularity all over the world. Famous operas and ballets, symphonies and songs have become classics. The great Russian composers successfully combined national forms with the technique and style of European music. Folk melodies very often were used in famous symphonies, operas and ballets.

Russian folk music has also gained great popularity not only domestically, but in many other countries of the world.

Russian music was acknowledged in the middle of the 19th century, after the success of Glinka's operas. In the late 1860s, five talented Russian composers, Balakirev, Borodin, Cui, Mussorgsky, and Rimsky-Korsakov, formed a group. They wrote in different styles but had common views concerning the development of Russian music. The peculiarity of the Russian ornamentalism was vividly shown in Borodin's opera "Prince Igor." Rimsky-Korsakov was known for developing national traditions of Russian folk music. The most original composer, Mussorgsky, wrote the outstanding historic opera "Boris Godunov." His musical achievements have been very important in the development of music in the 20th century.

The first music conservatories in Russia were founded on the initiative of Anton and Nikolai Rubinstein in St. Petersburg (1862) and in Moscow (1866). Many outstanding musicians and composers graduated from them. One of these was Peter Tchaikovsky. His masterpieces, opera "Eugene Onegin," ballets "Swan Lake," "Sleeping Beauty" and "The Nutcracker," won widespread international popularity, and are still enjoyed today.

In the beginning of the 20th century, due to the activity of the famous Russian artist Diaghilev, Russian music became well-known in the West. He staged Russian classics in Paris and introduced the original ballets of Igor Stravinsky to the western public. Diaghilev helped to foster the career of Prokofiev.

After the October revolution, many musicians left Russia, Prokofiev among them. He spent nearly 20 years abroad and returned to Russia in the mid-1930s. After his return he wrote his most famous works, including the ballet "Romeo and Juliet" and the orchestral fairy tale "Peter and the Wolf."

In the mid-1930s, music in the Soviet Union came under the control of the government-sponsored Union of Soviet Composers. In spite of accusations of "bourgeois formalism" (the worst artistic crime under Soviet rule) and strong suppression, the most talented composers, Khachaturian, Shostakovich, Prokofiev, created their prominent works.

In the changing situation of the 1960s the new avant-garde composers, Alfred Schnitke and Sofia Gubaidulina, began their struggle for modern expression in music. Their works were ignored by authorities. However, glasnost opened new opportunities for the development of different styles and movements in music.

Art and Architecture

In the early ages, Russian art and architecture were strongly influenced by the Byzantine style. This influence was weakened during the Tatar (Mongol) invasion. In the period beginning in the 14th century and continuing through the 17th century, Russian art had a religious character. The beautiful examples of early religious art are white-stone churches in Vladimir (a town east of Moscow) and icons of the 11th-12th centuries. During the Tatar's invasion, the icon painting schools moved to the north, to Novgorod and Pskov.

In the 14th-17th centuries the main religious art style began to change. Churches in Moscow at this time became more colorful. Multi-towered churches were built, such as the unique and magnificent Cathedral of Saint Basil in Moscow (1555-60). Icon paintings of this period are represented by the works of famous masters: Theophanes the Greek, Andrei Rublev, and Dionisius.

The westernization of Russian culture in the early 18th century was expressed first in the architecture of Saint Petersburg, the new capital of Russia. Two main styles of Western European art, baroque and rococo, are represented by buildings of this period. The most famous architect of this period, Bartolomeo Rastrelli, designed the well-known Winter Palace, Stroganov Palace at Nevsky Prospect, and the Summer Tsarist Palace in Pushkin (Tsarskoye Selo).

In the beginning of the 19th century the majority of the most important buildings in St. Petersburg were designed by Carlo Rossi. He completed the ensemble of the Winter Palace Square, designed the Senate and Synod buildings, Alexander Theater, and Mikhailovsky Palace (now the Russian Museum). The famous Kazan Cathedral was designed by the prominent Russian architect Voronikhin.

Early Russian painting is well represented by portrait painters Borovitsky and Levitsky, and later in the beginning of the 19th century by Kiprensky and Briullov.

The most famous group of Russian painters of the 19th century was known under the name of "Peredvizhniki" (the Wanderers), who worked in different genres, but their motto was realism. They organized an independent Association of Traveling Art Exhibits. The most prominent of these were: Kramskoi, Repin, Perov, Kuindzhi, Vereshchagin, and Vasnetsov.

At the turn of the 20th century, innovative and romantic painting styles gained popularity. A group of new painters and artists organized their own magazine "Mir Iskusstva" (World of Art). They created many achievements in European modern art. At the same time, new vanguard movements, such as cubism, futurism, and rayonism, created their first masterpieces. Later the names of Kandinsky, Malevich became well known to the whole world.

In the first years after the October Revolution of 1917, the vanguard artists actively participated in the new social life. Different styles existed in art and architecture, the most interesting of which was the constructivist style, represented by Melnikov.

The advent of 1932 found all artistic groups forbidden and the single style of socialist realism proclaimed. The best vanguard works of the period were never exhibited. In architecture the quasi-classical style became dominant, the best examples of these Stalinist era's pompous style are the buildings of the new Moscow University ensemble.

During the Khrushchev period, standardized constructions dominated the architecture, especially in mass housing. At the same time, the vanguard movement reappeared in painting. The new independent street exhibitions did not last very long, however.

During the Brezhnev period, after the exhibition of vanguard art was bulldozed in 1974, many artists emigrated from the country.

The situation changed after 1985, when glasnost and pluralism in art was proclaimed. One can now find different styles in art, and many exhibitions of formerly forbidden art works were organized in Russia. Talented artists now have an opportunity to exhibit their works openly.

EVERYDAY LIFE

I. Practical Advice

A. Location

Distance in Russia is expressed by meters and kilometers (1 meter = 3.3 feet; 1 kilometer = 0.6 miles).

In answering questions about direction, people will say to go straight ahead, left, right or back (not by north, east, south or west parameters). People will name the streets or the buildings by which you have to pass and where to turn or stop (not by blocks). They will give some specific landmarks such as large stores, cinemas, or distinguished buildings. If the distance is long they may suggest that you use some form of transportation.

B. Mass transportation

The most common way to reach your destination is by the extensive network of public transportation. The most comfortable and fastest form of transportation in large Russian cities, such as Moscow and St. Petersburg, is the subway (Metro). It may be overcrowded, especially during rush hours, but it connects all city regions in the shortest way. It is not very difficult to find your way around the Metro because of many maps and guiding signs. But it is preferable to look at the map and find the way to the station you need beforehand. It is easy to use the Metro map and to change trains. The sign for transferring train lines is "Переход." The most beautiful is the Moscow Metro. Cars leave at about two minute intervals. You must buy a token at the lobby to enter the Metro station. One token gives you the right to reach the station you need with as many line transfers as necessary.

If the location you desire is far from a Metro station it is possible to use other kinds of transportation: bus, trolley bus, tram, shuttle (route taxi). In large cities, shuttle stations are located near big shopping centers or Metro stations, and go in different directions, or they connect two or three big shopping centers. You may ask the driver to stop anywhere along the route and get out. To ride a shuttle you have to pay a set fee for one ride.

For short distances it is more convenient to take a bus, or a trolley bus, or a tram. You have to buy tickets in advance (generally it is a book of 10 tickets for 10 rides) or sometimes you can buy tickets from the driver. Tickets do not expire untill they are used. The passenger is responsible for validating them upon boarding the vehicle by using a hole punching device. Occasionally, a conductor will ask to see your ticket. Anyone travelling without a valid ticket will be fined.

You can use a train to go out of town, as well as to go from one area of town to another (if the town is large, like Moscow, for example). All railroads in Russia are state-owned. There are several main train stations in Moscow and St. Petersburg leading in different directions. You can always find the one you need if you call railroad information service, or at the travel agencies.

It is better to buy a ticket in advance, but for a regional trip you can buy tickets just before your departure. For these trips you can take an electric train. They leave the main station at about half hour intervals. For longer travels the long-distance trains may be used. These are equipped with meal cars ("vagon-restaran"). The quality of food is not very high. It is wise to take some snacks with you. However, a vendor will offer you hot tea, cookies and candies, and sometimes sandwiches and bottled water. Be prepared to share the compartment with other people, possibly of the opposite sex. If you want to have the whole compartment to yourself, you may buy all the tickets in your compartment. There are different classes of cars: international (or the first class) sleeper for 2 persons, sleeper for 4 persons, and general for more than 4 persons.

None of the previously mentioned methods of transportation are air-conditioned except international trains.

C. Taxi

You may want to hire a taxi, however, it is not as comfortable as in other countries. Sometimes it is difficult to find a taxi, or the driver may ask you to pay too much. Do not agree to pay more than 10-15 dollars for a long ride and 5 dollars for a short one. It is better to agree on a fee in advance. You can request a taxi at the hotel desk, but there will be an extra fee for this service.

D. Car rental

It is possible to rent a car in the state or private travel companies. But you have to remember that the traffic is very congested in large cities and it is very difficult to find a parking place. To buy gasoline may be a problem, and it is difficult and rather expensive to repair the car, if you leave the area where you rented the car. But if money is not a question for you, you can always find any kind of services at private repair stations or private repairmen (near gasoline stations).

F. Gasoline

In order to fill your rented car with gasoline, consider the following. Gas is sold by the liter. One US gallon equals 3.78 liters. There are fewer service stations than in the United States.

Fuel is classified by the octane rating as follows: 95 refers to Extra, 93 refers to Super, 76 refers to Normal. For foreign cars it is preferable to buy 95.

G. Traffic rules

There are slight differences in traffic rules, as well. You are not permitted to make a right turn on red under any circumstance. The rule of the right-of-way is very strictly enforced at intersections. You cannot cross the solid white line. Speed limit is marked in kilometers/hour. The limits are 80 km/h on highways and 60 in town. These limits, however, may be overridden by other posted speed limits.

Drunk driving is absolutely forbidden. There is not an allowable blood alcohol content level. If you test positive for any amount of alcohol, your driver's license may be confiscated on the spot. Pedestrians have a special crosswalk (wide white stripes across the street), where they have the right-of-way. But it is forbidden to cross the street in other than specially marked places or on red lights for pedestrians. A pedestrian may be fined for violation of this rule. If there is an underground tunnel nearby, it is mandatory to use it. A driver is not responsible for the life and health of the pedestrian who violates these rules.

In case of emergency, dial 02 for the police, 01 for the fire department, 03 for the ambulance service.

II. Currency

The official Russian currency is the ruble. One ruble equals 100 kopecks. You can exchange your hard currency at the airport exchange, at the Intourist hotels, at different banks in the large cities (a list of these banks and hard-currency rates are published in all business newspapers, and you may inquire about this in the hotel or in the embassies). The exchange of traveler's check may be done at the International bank, or at an office in foreign banks.

You cannot use your credit cards in Russian stores or in the majority of hotels. Be prepared to pay in cash. Hard currency is accepted only in special and private stores, not in state shops. Keep your receipts as you may have to show them to the custom officials upon leaving the country. Plan in advance how many of your dollars you want to exchange for rubles, to change them back may be more complicated.

III. Shopping

A. Food

There are different types of stores in Russia. Large state stores are usually specified as selling either food or consumer goods (food store - ГАСТРОНО́М; consumer goods store - УНИВЕРМА́Г). State stores are generally open from 8 a.m. to 8-9 p.m., most of them are closed on Sundays.

Smaller stores are nearly all privatized or, in many cities they are rented by the workers. They can have their own schedule. Small shops usually close for lunch, from 1 to 2 p.m. or from 2 to 3 p.m. There are not very many supermarkets in Russia and only a few of them offer 24 hour service.

If you want to buy fresh produce of higher quality, it is better to go to a farmer's market. Here you can buy fresh meat, honey, and flowers as well. Usually there are different small shops selling various foods (sausages, canned fruits and vegetables, deli, etc.) at the market place. If you are expecting guests and want to buy everything in one place, it is preferable to go to the market, however, prices are higher. You cannot buy bread in the market. It is better to go to a special bakery. Usually there is a department where you can buy sweet cakes, pies, cookies and candies.

Everything is sold by the metric unit of measure: 1 kilogram equals 2.2 lbs. , 1 liter equals 0.26 gallons.

2. Apparel

When shopping for clothes, it is necessary to know the Russian sizes, which are slightly different from those of the USA and Europe. These are approximate comparisons of Russian, European and American sizes:

For men and women - Russian 44, 46, 48, 50, 52, 54, 56; European - 38, 40, 42, 44, 46, 48, 50; American - 8, 10, 12, 14, 16, 18, extra large sizes.

The height is shown on a label in centimeters, for example women's short will be 152-158 cm., average - 160-168 cm., tall - 170-182 cm.; men's 164-170 cm., 172-178 cm., 180-188 cm.

Sizes for toddlers, children and teenagers are measured by height in centimeters.

A woman's shoe size 6 is approximately Russian size 35 or 36-37 European.

There are some world class stores in Moscow and St. Petersburg, but most of them are hard-currency stores. Prices in these stores are rather high, but you can buy fashionable and high quality European clothes, jewelry, make-up and souvenirs.

Recently, new joint ventures opened their own stores and supermarkets. They sell clothes for rubles as well as hard-currency.

When purchasing any electrical appliances, one must know that in Russia the standard voltage is 220. An adapter is required for an electrical device designed for 110 Volts.

IV. Restaurant

There are a lot of private cafes and restaurants in large Russian towns. Usually they are small, nicely decorated, and have a higher quality of service and meal. All Intourist and foreign companies' hotels have larger restaurants. Some of them accept only hard currency. These have better choices of meals and wider selections of wines, but prices may be higher, especially for those that provide variety shows. Some exotic restaurants are now opening (Indian, Chinese, Vietnamese, etc.), but do not expect them to exist in great numbers.

In some restaurants it is required to make reservations in advance and you have to wait to be seated. Very few restaurants have separate smoking and non-smoking sections.

It is not customary to serve iced water. Your cold drinks are prechilled and seldom served with ice cubes.

There can be vegetarian meals on the menu, and salads are usually served as the appetizer. Salad dressings may be different. They are generally mayonnaise or oil with vinegar and spices. The main meal is served around 1-2 p.m. It consists of salad, soup, main meal (usually meat dish), dessert (pastry, cake or ice-cream), and coffee or tea. When you pay your bill you may include your tip, or leave it on the table.

Let's list some Russian dishes you can try:

борщ	- borshch, beet soup;
щи	- shchi, cabbage soup;
пельме́ни	- pelmeni, ravioli with meat;
блины́	- bliny, thin pancakes;
пирожки́	- pirozhki, pastry cakes with meat, cabbage, jam, potatoes, or mushroom filling.

Before one starts eating, you can say "Прия́тного аппети́та!" (good appetite).

V. Introduction/Farewells

Greetings in Russia are more formal then in the United States. If you address people whom you don't know very well, it is better to use the formal polite greeting "Здра́вствуйте!" (Hello!). This greeting may be informal if the ending -те is dropped (Здра́вствуй). But you can use this form only to address children or very close friends. This is due to the difference between the two forms of the Russian pronoun "you." There are two forms of this pronoun, singular "ты" and plural "вы". The singular form is used only in informal conversation with one person, while the plural is used in formal conversation with one person or many people. As the imperative forms of the Russian verbs depend on the person whom you address, they take the polite/plural or informal version (with ending -те or without).

The general way of greeting is to use the time of the day. This is also the safe alternative when one is not sure whether or not the informal greeting is appropriate.

> До́брое у́тро! - Good morning!
> До́брый день! - Good day!
> До́брый ве́чер! - Good evening!
> До́брой но́чи! - Good night!

The word "До свида́ния!" expresses good-bye. It is also equivalent to the expression "See you soon."

There is an etiquette in introducing people to each other. Usually a younger person is introduced to an elder person, a lady to a gentleman and a subordinate to a superior. The same way is appropriate in handshaking.

VI. Visiting

The Russians are very hospitable and warm people. They like to have guests, in spite of shortages of money and difficulties in their everyday life. If you are invited to a Russian family, it is polite not to be later than 30 minutes. Small presents or flowers, candy, or a bottle of wine would be appreciated. But you can come empty handed as well. It is good to bring a small present, candy or chewing gum for children. Generally the hosts try to serve many different salads and appetizers first, but be careful, do not eat too much, because the main meal will come later, and usually it is rather rich. The Russians are considered to be wine and vodka lovers. It is true in some families. But do not be confused by this. You may always decline to drink alcohol, mentioning your health as an excuse.

VII. Communications

The communication system is rather good in Russia. You can use the telephone in your hotel to make long-distance calls, or ask the hotel service to connect you with the number you need. You can use long-distance service at post offices or the international communication service at the Central Telegraph. There is a special international post office, where you can send and receive your mail and packages. Public telephones operate by the insertion of a coin. Fax machines are available in all big hotels and at Central Telegraphs.

Many newspapers and magazines in English are available. These will be found at the hotels and there are some radio stations which broadcast news in English, as well.

VIII. Time

Russia uses military time, for example 7:30 p.m. will be 19 hours 30 minutes.

The first day of the week is Monday. Here are some words and expressions, connected with the time and calendar:

Days of the week:

Понеде́льник	- Monday
Вто́рник	- Tuesday
Среда́	- Wednesday
Четве́рг	- Thursday
Пя́тница	- Friday
Суббо́та	- Saturday
Воскресе́нье	- Sunday

Months of the year:

Янва́рь	- January
Февра́ль	- February
Март	- March
Апре́ль	- April
Май	- May
Ию́нь	- June
Ию́ль	- July
А́вгуст	- August
Сентя́брь	- September
Октя́брь	- October
Ноя́брь	- November
Дека́брь	- December

Asking for time: Кото́рый час? Ско́лько вре́мени? - What time is it?

Time of the day:

У́тро	- morning
По́лдень	- noon

День	- afternoon
Ве́чер	- evening
Ночь	- night

LANGUAGE LESSONS

PRONUNCIATION GUIDE

Alphabet

The Russian alphabet consists of 33 signs, or letters, of which two Ь and Ъ have no sound value: they make the consonant before them either soft or hard. The alphabet is called Cyrillic, and is used by several other Slavic nations. It is a combination of Greek, Latin, and purely Slavic letters. The sounds which had no precise equivalent in Greek or Latin were invented by two South Slavic monks, Cyrill and Methodius, in the 9th century. Some letters have the same sound as the English; others look the same, but have a different sound in Russian.

Vowels

There are 5 basic vowels plus their 5 "soft equivalents," which means that the sound "y" (as in "yes") precedes the vowel.

Russian - English	Russian - English
А, а - a as in f<u>a</u>r	Я, я - ya as in <u>ya</u>rd
О, о - o as in l<u>o</u>ng	Ё, ё - yo as in <u>Yo</u>rk
Ы, ы - i as in s<u>i</u>t	И, и - ee as in s<u>ee</u>n
Э, э - e as in <u>e</u>nd	Е, е - ye as in <u>ye</u>t
У, у - oo as in b<u>oo</u>th	Ю, ю - u as in <u>you</u>

The two soundless signs Ь and Ъ have been mentioned above.

Consonants

Russian - English	Russian - English
Б, б - B as in <u>b</u>oy	П, п - P as in <u>p</u>al
В, в - V as in <u>v</u>oice	Р, р - R (rolled and pure as in Spanish)
Г, г - G as in <u>g</u>lad	С, с - S as in <u>s</u>un
Д, д - D as in <u>d</u>og	Т, т - T as in <u>t</u>wo
Ж, ж - ZH as in mea<u>s</u>ure	Ф, ф - F as in <u>f</u>riend

З, з - Z as in <u>z</u>inc
Й, й - Y as in ma<u>y</u>
К, к - K as in <u>k</u>ing
Л, л - L as in <u>l</u>ord

М, м - M as in <u>m</u>ind

Н, н - N as in <u>n</u>o

Ц, ц - TS as in i<u>ts</u>
Ч, ч - CH as in <u>ch</u>eck
Ш, ш - SH as in <u>sh</u>ow
Щ, щ - SHCH as in fre<u>sh sh</u>allots

Х, х - KH or as German CH
a<u>ch</u>

The Russian alphabet

А а, Б б, В в, Г г, Д д, Е е, Ё ё, Ж ж, З з, И и, Й й, К к, Л л, М м, Н н, О о, П п, Р р, С с, Т т, У у, Ф ф, Х х, Ц ц, Ч ч, Ш ш, Щ щ, ъ, Ы ы, ь, Э э, Ю ю, Я я

Rules of Russian pronunciation

1.   The Russian alphabet has hard and soft consonants. To make a consonant soft requires either a soft sigh ь or a soft vowel, i.e. the "yo," "ye," etc. after the consonant. Only 6 letters are excluded: ч, щ, й are always soft, and ж, ш, ц are always hard, no matter what follows them.

<u>Exa</u>mple: те, ти, ть are soft, while т, ты, та are hard.

2.   Accent or stress.
As does English, Russian has free stress, that is the accent can fall anywhere, on any syllable in any word. As in English language the word *"machine"* is stressed on the "i," so the Russian маши́на also is stressed on "и." Stresses in the two languages, unlike the above word, seldom coincide, but can be found more often in cognates. That is in words like the one above, which are identical in both languages.

<u>Example</u>: medicine - медици́на, ballet - бале́т. Accent/stress marks are given in all dialogs, vocabulary and examples, in all words having more than one vowel. If you see a word with letter ё, stress is always on that letter.

3. Unstressed vowels.

Unstressed vowels in Russian are pronounced less distinctly than vowels in stressed syllables. In pronouncing o and e a strict rule must be observed. If ó is stressed it is pronounced as pure o. If it is unstressed it is pronounced as Russian **a**. Unstressed e is pronounced as **и**, stressed is pure e.

<u>Examples:</u> Россия - [ra-ssee-ya], аэропóрт - [a-e-ra-port], самолёт - [sa-ma-lyot], женá - [zhee-na], простите - [pra-stee-tee].

LESSON ONE. УРОК ПЕ́РВЫЙ.

Встреча

Ивано́вы Никола́й Никола́евич и А́нна Степа́новна, гра́ждане США, эмигри́ровали из Росси́и 35 лет наза́д, е́дут в делову́ю пое́здку в Росси́ю.

Орло́вы Серге́й Миха́йлович и Татья́на Льво́вна, тури́сты, бы́ли в США оди́н ме́сяц.
О́бе па́ры ру́сские.

Самолёт то́лько что пересёк росси́йскую грани́цу. Две па́ры сидя́т в одно́м ряду́.

Орло́в:	Прости́те. Всё в поря́дке? Вы поса́дки бои́тесь?
Ивано́ва:	Спаси́бо, всё в поря́дке. Я уе́хала из Росси́и три́дцать пять лет наза́д и возвраща́юсь туда́ пе́рвый раз.
Орло́ва:	Почему́ вы сейча́с возвраща́етесь? У вас там ро́дственники?
Ивано́в:	Нет, на́ша пое́здка делова́я, но мы хоти́м уви́деть всю страну́. Но дава́йте познако́мимся. Меня́ зову́т Никола́й Никола́евич Ивано́в, а э́то моя́ жена́ А́нна Степа́новна.
Орло́в:	Серге́й Миха́йлович Орло́в, а э́то моя́ жена́ Татья́на Льво́вна. Мы живём в Москве́. Е́здили в Аме́рику как тури́сты.
Ивано́ва:	А кто вы по профе́ссии?
Орло́в:	Татья́на - учи́тельница, а я - врач. А чем вы занима́етесь?
Ивано́в:	А́нна рабо́тает в ба́нке, а мы с сы́ном прода́ём компью́теры. У вас есть де́ти?

Орло́ва:	Да, сын и дочь. Они́ хо́дят в шко́лу. Сейча́с ба́бушка за ни́ми смо́трит. Я уве́рена, что они́ ждут нас в аэропорту́.
Ивано́ва:	Смотри́те, мы уже́ приземля́емся.

LESSON ONE

Meeting people / Introduction

The Ivanovs, Nikolai Nikolaevich and Anna Stepanovna, US citizens visiting Russia on a business trip, emigrated from Russia 35 years ago.

The Orlovs, Sergei Mikhailovich and Tatiana L'vovna, Russian tourists returning from a visit to the USA, where they spent one month. Both couples are Russian.

A plane just crossed the Russian border. The two couples sit in the same row.

Orlov: (Sergei)	Excuse me. Is everything all right? Are you afraid of landing?
Ivanova: (Anna)	Thank you. Everything is fine. I left Russia thirty five years ago and I am returning there for the first time.
Orlova: (Tatiana)	Why are you returning now? Do you have relatives there?
Ivanov: (Nikolai)	No, our trip is a business trip, and we want to see the whole country. But let us introduce ourselves. My name is Nikolai Nikolaevich Ivanov, and this is my wife Anna Stepanovna.
Orlov:	Sergei Mikhailovich Orlov, and this is my wife Tatiana L'vovna. We live in Moscow.
Ivanova:	What are your professions?
Orlov:	Tatiana is a teacher, and I am a doctor. And what are your occupations?
Ivanov:	Anna works in a bank, and I and my son sell computers. Do you have any children?

Orlova: Yes, a son and a daughter. They go to
            school. Now their grandmother is taking
            care of them. I am sure they are waiting
            for us at the airport.

Ivanova: Look! We are already landing.

VOCABULARY

уро́к	lesson	лет (год)	years (year)
пе́рвый	first	наза́д	ago
гра́ждане	citizens	и	and
США	USA	возвраща́юсь	(I) return
эмигри́ровали	emigrated	туда́	(to) there
(из) Росси́и	(from) Russia	в ... раз	for ... time
пое́здка	trip	почему́	why
делова́я	business (adj.)	сейча́с	now
бы́ли	were	у вас	you have
оди́н	one	там	there
ме́сяц	month	ро́дственники	relatives
о́бе	both	нет	no
па́ра	couple	на́ша	our
ру́сские	Russian (plural)	но	but
		мы	we
встре́ча	meeting	хоти́м	(we) want
самолёт	airplane	уви́деть	see
то́лько что	just now	всю	all/whole
пересёк	crossed	страна́	country
росси́йскую	of Russia	дава́йте	let's
грани́ца	border	познако́мимся	get acquainted
две па́ры	two couples	меня́ зову́т	my name is
сидя́т	sit	а	and/but
в одно́м ряду́	in the same row	э́то	this (is)
одна́	one	моя́	my (feminine)
же́нщина	woman	жена́	wife
не́рвничает	is nervous	живём	(we) live
поса́дка	landing	в	in/to
прости́те	excuse me	Москва́	Moscow
вы	you	е́здили	went/traveled
бо́йтесь	afraid	Аме́рика	America
спаси́бо	thank you	как	as/like
я	I	тури́ст	tourist
уе́хала	left	кто	who
из	from	по	by
три́дцать пять	35	профе́ссия	profession
		учи́тельница	teacher
		врач	doctor

рабо́тает	works	ба́бушка	grandmother
банк	bank	за ни́ми	after them
с	with	смо́трит	looks
сын	son	уве́рена	sure/certain
продаём	sell	что	that/what
компью́тер	computer	ждут	wait
у вас есть	you have	нас	us
де́ти	children	аэропо́рт	airport
дочь	daughter	смотри́те	look (command)
они́	they		
хо́дят	go	уже́	already
шко́ла	school	приземля́емся	are landing

Expressions:

Прости́те. - Excuse me.

Спаси́бо. - Thank you.

Всё в поря́дке. - Everything is all right

Дава́йте познако́мимся. - Let us introduce ourselves.

Меня́ зову́т ... - My name is ...

Кто вы по профе́ссии? - What are your professions?

Чем вы занима́етесь? - What is your occupation?

Мы живём в Москве́. - We live in Moscow.

GRAMMAR

1. There are no articles in Russian. For example, the phrase: <u>I am a doctor</u>, will be translated as: Я врач. <u>This is the airport.</u> - Это аэропо́рт.

2. The verb **to be (I am, you are, etc.)**, быть (есть), is not used in the present tense in Russian. Only very seldom and mainly in scientific writing would this verb occur, or it may be used to stress the possession of something or the existence of something (Do you have children? - У вас есть де́ти?).

<u>Examples:</u>

This is my wife. - Э́то моя́ жена́.
Tatiana is a teacher. - Татья́на - учи́тельница.

3. Russian nouns (words like airplane, wife, morning) belong to different genders. There are three genders in Russian: masculine, feminine and neuter, like in German or French. This is not related to the human gender alone, but also depends on the noun endings in their nominative form. Thus "airplane" (самолёт) is masculine and referred to with the pronoun "he" (он). The word "wife" (жена́) is feminine as well as "meeting" (встре́ча). They are referred to as "she" (она́). The word "morning" (у́тро) is neuter and is referred to as "it" (оно́). You can determine the gender of Russian nouns from the ending in the nominative case (the case of subject):
a. If the noun ends in a consonant, in **й**, or sometimes in **ь** it is masculine.
b. If the noun ends in **а, я, ия** and sometimes in **ь**, it is feminine.
c. If the noun ends in **о, е, ие**, it is neuter.
d. Plural endings of Russian nouns are usually **и, ы**, and in some cases **а, я**.

Exercises:

1. Read Dialogue 1. Try to pronounce all sounds according to the rules.

2. What are the genders of the following nouns:
    встре́ча, самолёт, Росси́я, тури́ст, профе́ссия, страна́.

3. Translate into Russian:
    I am a doctor.
    My wife is a teacher.
    This is the airport.
    Thank you, everything is all right.
    This is my wife.

4. Memorize Dialogue 1.

УРОК ВТОРОЙ

Приезд в Москву

Орло́в:	Никола́й Никола́евич, вы мо́жете получи́ть свой бага́ж вот здесь. А там прове́рка паспорто́в.
Ивано́в:	Большо́е спаси́бо.
Офице́р:	Здра́вствуйте. Покажи́те, пожа́луйста, ваш паспо́рт. У вас ру́сские фами́лии. Вы говори́те по-ру́сски?
Ивано́в:	Коне́чно, мы здесь родили́сь.
Офице́р:	Как до́лго вы бу́дете здесь и где остано́витесь?
Ивано́ва:	Мы бу́дем здесь две неде́ли, в гости́нице "Метропо́ль".
Офице́р:	Большо́е спаси́бо. Тепе́рь, пожа́луйста, пройди́те на тамо́жню.

Тамо́жня

Тамо́женник:	До́брое у́тро. Есть ли у вас ве́щи для предъявле́ния тамо́жне?
Ивано́в:	Нет, у нас то́лько ме́лкие пода́рки.
Тамо́женник:	Я хочу́ посмотре́ть э́тот чемода́н. Бу́дьте добры́, откро́йте его́.
Ивано́в:	Коне́чно. Вот, пожа́луйста.
Тамо́женник:	Всё в поря́дке. Спаси́бо. Жела́ю вам прия́тно провести́ вре́мя в на́шей стране́. До свида́ния.

LESSON TWO

Arrival at Moscow

Orlov: Nikolai Nikolaevich, you can pick up your luggage right here. And over there is the passport check.

Ivanov: Thank you very much.

Officer: Hello! May I see your passport? Your names are Russian. Do you speak Russian?

Ivanov: Of course. We were born here.

Officer: How long will you stay here and where are you staying?

Ivanova: We'll be here two weeks in the hotel "Metropol."

Officer: Thank you very much. Now, go to customs, please.

Customs

Customs officer: Good morning. Have you anything to declare?

Ivanov: No. We brought only small gifts.

Customs officer: I would like to see this suitcase. Please, could you open it for me?

Ivanov: Of course. Here you are.

Customs officer: Everything is all right, thank you. Have a nice time in our country. Good bye!

VOCABULARY

второй	second	гостиница	hotel
приезд	arrival	теперь	now
можете	you can/may	пройдите	go
получить	receive/pick up		(command)
		таможня	customs
багаж	luggage	таможенник	customs officer
здесь	here		
проверка	check	вещь	thing
паспорт	passport	для	for
офицер	officer	предъявление	declaration
здравствуйте	Hello	у нас	we have
покажите	show (command)	только	only
		мелкие	small
пожалуйста	please	подарки	gifts
ваш	your	я хочу	I want
русские	Russian (pl.)	посмотреть	to see
фамилия	last name	этот	this
говорите	(you) speak	чемодан	suitcase
по-русски	in Russian	будьте добры	be so kind
конечно	sure/certainly	откройте	open (command)
родились	are born		
как долго	how long	его	it
будете	you will	желаю вам	(I) wish you
где	where	приятно	nice/pleasant
остановитесь	you'll stay	провести	spend
будем	(we) shell	время	time
неделя	week	нашей	our

Expressions:

Есть ли у вас? - Do you have?
Большое спасибо! - Thank you very much!
Здравствуйте. - Hello!
Покажите, пожалуйста, ваш паспорт. - May I see your passport, please.
Вы говорите по-русски? - Do you speak Russian?

Как до́лго вы бу́дете здесь? - How long will you stay here?

Пожа́луйста, пройди́те... - Please, go to ...

До́брое у́тро! - Good morning.

Жела́ю вам прия́тно провести́ вре́мя. - Have a nice time.

GRAMMAR

1. Russian is known as a highly inflected language. This means the endings of the words change; this is true for nouns, adjectives, verbs, etc. Since there are six cases, the relationship of words in a sentence is conveyed by the endings. The word order, therefore, is not as important in Russian as in English. Consider this sentence: "I very much want home to go." At the least, this sounds awkward, and ungrammatical, but would be an acceptable word order in Russian. Words in a sentence can be shifted around in Russian, even for emphasis, and the endings of these words will make the sentence understandable.

2. The six cases are:

Nominative - the subject case. The word has only the gender ending attached to it, and appears the way it is in the dictionary.

Genitive - indicates possession, as "the child's book," "University of Colorado," "Book cover, i.e., the cover of the book." It is used also with prepositions, with some verbs, in time expressions, with numbers, etc.

Dative - the indirect object case; the English preposition "to" carries the idea of the indirect object, as "I gave this letter to him." It is also used with other prepositions.

Accusative - direct object case. Using the same sentence: "I gave this letter to him," "this letter" is the direct object. It is used with prepositions, indicating a direction of moving: "I go to school." It can be used with other prepositions.

Instrumental - indicates the instrument of some action: "I ride the bus." "Bus" is the instrument of your transportation. "Please, write with this pen," here "pen" is the tool or instrument of your action. Prepositions are also used with this case.

Prepositional (or Locative) - used only with prepositions, primarily shows locations: "In the hotel," "At the meeting."

It is not important for our purpose to memorize the prepositions, or the various case endings. As you memorize the dialogues, it would be good idea just to note the prepositions used and the changing endings.

Exercises:

1. Read Dialogue 2. Pay attention to the noun endings.

2. Translate into Russian:

> Hello! Good morning!
> Thank you very much.
> Good bye.
> Have a nice time.

3. Memorize Dialogue 2.

УРО́К ТРЕ́ТИЙ

Такси́

Орло́вы встреча́ют свои́х дете́й и ба́бушку у вы́хода.

Де́вочка:	Ма́ма, как дела́?
Орло́ва:	Отли́чно. Мы встре́тили о́чень ми́лую па́ру в самолёте. Вы ско́ро их уви́дите. Мы пригласи́ли их на обе́д на сле́дующей неде́ле.
Орло́в:	Дава́йте пое́дем домо́й. Вот стоя́нка такси́.

В такси́.

Шофёр:	До́брое у́тро. Куда́ е́дем?
Орло́в:	У́лица Го́голя, дом со́рок пять. Вы зна́ете, где э́то?
Шофёр:	Да, недалеко́ от це́нтра го́рода. Но я ду́маю, вам нужны́ две маши́ны. У вас сли́шком мно́го багажа́ и пять челове́к. Все в одно́ такси́ не ся́дете.
Орло́в:	Да, пра́вда. Татья́на, ты поезжа́й с детьми́. До́ма уви́димся.

— — —

Орло́в:	Нам повезло́, нет у́личных про́бок. Останови́тесь здесь, пожа́луйста. Вот э́то наш дом. Ско́лько с меня́? (Ско́лько я вам до́лжен?)
Шофёр:	На счётчике четы́реста пятьдеся́т рубле́й.
Орло́в:	Вот вам пятьсо́т. Сда́чи не на́до. До свида́ния.

LESSON 3

Taxi

The Orlovs met their children and grandmother at the exit.

The girl:	How are you, mom?
Orlova:	Perfect. We met a very nice couple on the plane. You'll see them soon. We invited them to dinner next week.
Orlov:	Well, let's go home. There is a taxi stand.

In the taxi.

Driver:	Good morning. Where would you like to go?
Orlov:	45, Gogol Street. Do you know where it is?
Driver:	Yes. It is not far from downtown. But I think you will need two cars. You have too much luggage and five people. It will not all fit in one taxi.
Orlov:	That's true. Tatiana, you go with the children. See you at home.

— — —

Orlov:	We were lucky; no traffic jams. Please, stop here. This is our house. How much is it? (How much do I owe you?)
Driver:	The taximeter shows 450 rubles.
Orlov:	Here you are, there are 500 rubles. Keep the change. Good bye.

VOCABULARY.

тре́тий	third	вам нужны́	you need
такси́	taxi	маши́на	car
встреча́ют	meet	сли́шком	too
свои́х	their	мно́го	much/many
дете́й	children	челове́к	persons
у	near	все	everybody
вы́ход	exit	одно́	one (neuter)
де́вочка	girl	не	not
ма́ма	mom	ся́дете	(you'll) sit
де́ло	matter	пра́вда	true
отли́чно	perfect	поезжа́й	go (command)
встре́тили	met		
о́чень	very	до́ма	at home
ми́лую	nice	уви́димся	we'll meet
ско́ро	soon	нам повезло́	we are lucky
их	them	нет	no
уви́дите	(you'll) see	у́личных про́-	traffic jams
пригласи́ли	invited	бок	stop (com-
на обе́д	for dinner	останови́тесь	mand)
на сле́ду-	next	наш	our
ющей неде́ле	week	ско́лько	how much
пое́дем	(we'll) go	с	from
домо́й	(to) home	меня́	me
стоя́нка	stop/station	до́лжен	owe
шофёр	driver	счётчик	taximeter
куда́	(to) where	четы́реста	400
е́дем	(we are) going	пятьдеся́т	50
у́лица	street	рубле́й	rubles
дом	house	(рубль)	(ruble)
со́рок пять	45	пятьсо́т	500
зна́ете	(you) know	сда́ча	change
да	yes	не	not
недалеко́ от	not far from	на́до	need
центр го́рода	downtown	пла́тье	dress
ду́маю	(I) think	свида́ние	meeting

Expressions:

Как дела? - How are you?
Давайте поедем домой. - Let's go home.
Вот стоянка такси. - Here is a taxi stand.
Вы знаете, где это? - Do you know, where it is?
Нам повезло. - We are lucky.
Сколько с меня? Сколько я вам должен? Сколько платить? -
How much do I owe you? How much is it?
С вас ... - You owe me ...
Сдачи не надо. - Keep the change.

Extra words for local transportation:

Автобус - bus;
троллейбус - trolley bus;
трамвай - tram;
поезд - train;
метро - Metro.

GRAMMAR

Endings of six Russian noun cases are:

Case	Masculine	Feminine	Neuter
Nominative	банк сын Сергей рубль	жена́ неде́ля Росси́я дочь	у́тро пла́тье (dress) свида́ние (meeting)
Genitive	ба́нка сы́на Серге́я рубля́	жены́ неде́ли Росси́и до́чери	утра́ пла́тья свида́ния
Dative	ба́нку сы́ну Серге́ю рублю́	жене́ неде́ле Росси́и до́чери	утру́ пла́тью свида́нию
Accusative	банк сы́на (animated) Серге́я (-"-) рубль	жену́ неде́лю Росси́ю дочь	у́тро пла́тье свида́ние
Instrumental	ба́нком сы́ном Сеге́ем рублём	жено́й неде́лей Росси́ей до́черью	у́тром пла́тьем свида́нием
Prepositional	ба́нке сы́не Серге́е рубле́	жене́ неде́ле Росси́и до́чери	у́тре неде́ле свида́нии

1. Pay attention to two forms of the accusative case: <u>masculine</u> nouns indicating things (<u>inanimate</u> nouns) in <u>accusative</u> has the same ending as in the <u>nominative</u>; for persons and animals (<u>animate</u> nouns) it has the

same ending as in <u>genitive</u>.

2. Neuter with ending -ие and feminine nouns with soft sign (ь) at the end, and ending -ия in nominative case have different endings (look at the table).

Exercises:

1. Read Dialogue 3.

2. Try to find nouns in different cases.

3. Translate into Russian:

> How are you? - Perfect.
> Let's go home.
> Do you know where it is?
> Stop here, please.
> How much is it? Keep the change.

4. Try to indicate the case of nouns in the following sentences:

> Мы встре́тили ба́бушку у вы́хода.
> Прове́рка паспорто́в там.
> Мы в гости́нице.
> Я хочу́ посмотре́ть чемода́н.

5. Memorize Dialogue 3.

УРÓК ЧЕТВЁРТЫЙ

Гостѝница

Иванóвы тóлько что приéхали в гостѝницу "Метропóль".

Иванóв:	Здрáвствуйте. Моё ѝмя - Николáй Николáевич Иванóв. Я закáзывал кóмнату на двоѝх из Нью-Йóрка.
Администрáтор:	Да, господѝн Иванóв. Запóлните эти анкéты. Спасѝбо. Вот ваш ключ. Нóмер двéсти дéсять. Это на вторóм этажé. Лифт напрáво, рядом с лéстницей. Ваш багáж сейчáс принесýт в нóмер.
Иванóв:	Где мóжно постáвить машѝну?
Администрáтор:	Под гостѝницей есть стоянка.
Иванóва:	Скажѝте, пожáлуйста, когдá и где мóжно позáвтракать? Я слышала, что зáвтрак вхóдит в стóимость нóмера.
Администрáтор:	Да. Ресторáн вот здесь, напрóтив бáра. Зáвтраки с семѝ до десятѝ утрá. Éсли хотѝте, мóжете заказáть зáвтрак в нóмер.
Иванóва:	Какѝе ещё услýги есть в гостѝнице?
Администрáтор:	У нас есть парикмáхерская, пóчта, магазѝн подáрков, обмéн валюты - это на пéрвом этажé. Бассéйн и спортзáл в подвáле. Éсли вам чтонибýдь нýжно, дáйте нам знать.

LESSON FOUR

Hotel

The Ivanovs have just arrived at the hotel "Metropol."

Ivanov: Hello! My name is Nikolai Nikolaevich Ivanov. I have reserved a room for two from New York.

Clerk: Yes, Mr. Ivanov. Please, fill out these forms. Thank you. Here is your key. The room is 210. This is on the second floor. The elevator is to the right, next to the stairs. Your luggage will be brought to your room right away.

Ivanov: Where can we park the car?

Clerk: There is an underground parking lot.

Ivanova: Could you tell me, please, where can we have breakfast? I heard it is included in the price of the room.

Clerk: The restaurant is right here, opposite the bar. Breakfast is served from 7 to 10 a.m. If you wish, you can order room service.

Ivanova: What other services do you have in the hotel?

Clerk: We have a hair salon, post office, gift shop, and currency exchange office on the first floor. The swimming pool and the health club are in the basement. If you need anything, please let us know.

VOCABULARY

четвёртый	fourth	напро́тив	in front of
прие́хали	arrived	бар	bar
и́мя	name	с семи́	from 7
моё	my (neutral)	до десяти́	to 10
зака́зывал	ordered	утра́	in the morning
ко́мната	room	попроси́ть	ask for
на двои́х	for two	за́втрак	breakfast
администра́тор	clerk	что́бы	to
господи́н	Mister	принести́	bring
запо́лните	fill out	каки́е	what kind
анке́та	forms	ещё	else
ключ	key	услу́га	service
но́мер	room number	парикма́херская	hair salon
две́сти де́сять	210	по́чта	post office
на	on	магази́н	shop/store
эта́ж	floor	пода́рков	(of) gifts
лифт	elevator	обме́н валю́ты	currency exchange
напра́во	to the right	бассе́йн	swimming pool
ря́дом (с)	next to	подва́л	basement
ле́стница	staircase	е́сли	if
принесу́т	(they'll) bring	что-нибу́дь	something
сейча́с	now	ну́жно	necessary
поста́вить	place/put/park	да́йте нам знать	let us know
под	under	рабо́тать	work
есть	there is/are	говори́ть	speak/talk
стоя́нка	parking lot	ты	you (familiar)
скажи́те	tell me	он	he
когда́	when	она́	she
поза́втракать	have breakfast	оно́	it
слы́шать	hear	вы	you (plural or polite)

часть	part	мы	we
стóимость	price	онú	they

Expressions:

Моё úмя ... - My first name is ...
Моя́ фамúлия ... - My last name is ...
Заполните э́ти анке́ты. - Fill out these forms.
Ваш но́мер на второ́м этаже́. - Your room is on the second floor.
Где мо́жно поста́вить маши́ну? - Where can I park the car?
Éсли вам что-нибу́дь ну́жно, да́йте нам знать. - If you need something, let us know.
Я слы́шал (слы́шала), что ... - I heard (in masculine and feminine forms) that...
Скажи́те, пожа́луйста ... - Could you tell me, please ...

Extra words

пообе́дать - have dinner/lunch
поу́жинать - have supper
валю́та - currency

GRAMMAR

The Russian verb system

1. There are two conjugations (the way verbs change for each personal pronoun), and irregular verbs, which have to be memorized individually.

The personal pronouns are:

Singular			Plural	
I	я	we	мы
you	ты (familiar)	you	вы (polite)
he, she, it	он, она́, оно́	they	они́

2. First conjugation verbs have these endings:

Second conjugation verbs have these endings:

работать - to work		говори́ть - to speak	
я	рабо́таю	я	говорю́
ты	рабо́таешь	ты	говори́шь
он, она́, оно́	рабо́тает	он, она́, оно́	говори́т
мы	рабо́таем	мы	говори́м
вы	рабо́таете	вы	говори́те
они́	рабо́тают	они́	говоря́т

The distinction in these conjugations lies in the usage of -e- in the first conjugation in second person singular, and up to the third plural, which have -ут/ют at the end. In the second conjugation the second person singular has **-и-** and the same letter in the endings up to the third person plural, where the ending is -ат/ят. The infinitive (that is the dictionary form of the verb) of the second conjugation has **-и-** in the ending, except for the irregular verbs. If there are other vowels in the ending of the verb, it is of the first conjugation.

Exercises:

1. Read Dialogue 4.

2. Translate into Russian:

> Do you speak Russian?
> I work in the bank.
> Could you tell me, please, where the currency exchange is?
> I speak Russian.

3. Memorize Russian personal pronouns.

4. Memorize Dialogue 4.

УРÓК ПЯ́ТЫЙ

Пóчта. Как пройти́?

Ивановы хотя́т посла́ть пи́сьма домо́й.

Иванóва:	Прости́те, вы не скáжете, где пóчта?
Прохóжий:	Пройди́те тудá. Иди́те пря́мо по у́лице до пéрвого светофóра. Там поверни́те налéво и на вторóм перекрёстке напрáво. Пóчта - трéтий дом слéва. Но вы мóжете доéхать на трамвáе. Нóмер шесть. Пéрвая остановка бу́дет музéй. Вторáя - большóй гастронóм. Там вам ну́жно сойти́. Э́то бу́дет пря́мо напрóтив пóчты.
Иванóва:	Спаси́бо.

На пóчте.

Иванóв:	Дóбрый день. Мы хоти́м посла́ть пи́сьма в Амéрику.
Слу́жащая:	Подойди́те, пожáлуйста, к трéтьему окóшку. Здесь тóлько посы́лки.
Иванóв:	Скóлько стóит посла́ть э́ти пи́сьма в Нью-Йóрк авиапóчтой?
Слу́жащая:	Сначáла мне нáдо их взвéсить. Э́то бу́дет стóить шестьсóт двáдцать рублéй и пятьдеся́т копéек.
Иванóв:	Спаси́бо. Когдá их полу́чат?
Слу́жащая:	Чéрез недéлю.
Иванóва:	Спаси́бо. Всегó хорóшего.

LESSON FIVE

Post Office. Asking for Directions.

The Ivanovs want to send letters home.

Ivanova: Excuse me, could you tell us where the post office is?

Pedestrian: Go over to this place. Go straight on this street to the first stop light. Turn to the left and at the second intersection turn to the right. The post office is the third building on the left. But you can also get there on the tram. Use number 6. The first stop is the Museum. The second is a large supermarket. You have to get off there and you will be directly across from the post office.

Ivanova: Thank you.

At the post office.

Ivanov: Good afternoon. We would like to send some letters to America.

Clerk: Please, go to the third window. This one is for packages only.

Ivanov: How much does it cost to send these letters to New York by airmail?

Clerk: I have to weigh them first. This will cost 620 rubles and 50 kopeks.

Ivanov: Thank you. When are they going to get them?

Clerk: In a week.

Ivanova: Thank you. All the best to you.

VOCABULARY

пя́тый	fifth	тре́тьему	third
как	how	око́шко	window
пройти́	go to	посы́лки	packages
хоте́ть	want	ско́лько сто́ит	how much
посла́ть	send		
сказа́ть	say/tell	э́ти	these
письмо́ (-а)	letter(s)	авиапо́чтой	by airmail
прохо́жий	pedestrian	снача́ла	first
иди́те	go (command)	мне на́до	I need
		их	them
пря́мо	straight	взве́сить	weigh
по	along, by	бу́дет сто́ить	will cost
до	until	шестьсо́т	600
светофо́р	street light	два́дцать	20
поверни́те	turn (command)	копе́ек	kopeks
		полу́чат	(they) will receive
нале́во	to the left		
перекрёсток	crossroads	че́рез неде́лю	in/after a week
сле́ва	from the left		
мо́жете, мочь	(you) may	всего́ хоро́шего	all the best
дое́хать	reach		
шесть	six	до́лжен,-на́, -ны́	must
остано́вка	stop		
бу́дет, быть	will, to be	жить	live
музе́й	museum	люби́ть	like/love
большо́й	big/large	е́хать	drive/ride
гастроно́м	food store	идти́	go (on foot)
вам ну́жно	you need	есть	eat
сойти́	get off	пить	drink
до́брый день	good day	покупа́ть	buy
слу́жащая	clerk (in office)	знать	know
		приглаша́ть	invite
подойди́те к	come up to (command)	на́до	need
		ну́жно	need

Expressions:

Вы не скáжете, как пройти ... ? - Could you tell me, how to get
(go) ... ?
Идúте прямо/налéво/напрáво. - Go straight/left/right.
Поверните налéво/напрáво. - Turn left/right.
Вы мóжете доéхать на трамвáе (автóбусе, троллéйбусе, метрó).
- You can go by tram (bus, trolley bus, metro).
Скóлько стóит? - How much is it?
Дóбрый день. - Good day.
Всегó хорóшего. - All the best.

GRAMMAR

1. Frequently used verbs, regular and irregular:

to live - жить	живу́ живём	живёшь живёте	живёт живу́т
to like/love - люби́ть	люблю́ лю́бим	лю́бишь лю́бите	лю́бит лю́бят
to drive/ride - éхать	éду éдем	éдешь éдете	éдет éдут
to walk/go (on foot) - идти́	иду́ идём	идёшь идёте	идёт иду́т
to eat - есть	ем еди́м	ешь еди́те	ест едя́т
to drink - пить	пью пьём	пьёшь пьёте	пьёт пью́т
to buy - покупа́ть	покупа́ю покупа́ем	покупа́ешь покупа́ете	покупа́ет покупа́ют
to know - знать	зна́ю зна́ем	зна́ешь зна́ете	зна́ет зна́ют
to invite - приглаша́ть	приглаша́ю приглаша́ем	пригла-ша́ешь приглаша́-ете	приглаша́ет приглаша́ют
to be - быть (future tense)	бу́ду бу́дем	бу́дешь бу́дете	бу́дет бу́дут

2. Modals (verbs used to express ability, need, wish):

can - мочь	могу́ мо́жем	мо́жешь мо́жете	мо́жет мо́гут
must - до́лжен	Я, ты, он до́лжен (masculine)	Я, ты, она́ должна́ (feminine)	Вы, они́ должны́
need - на́до (the same as ну́жно)	мне на́до нам на́до	тебе́ на́до вам на́до	ему́, ей на́до им на́до
want - хоте́ть	хочу́ хоти́м	хо́чешь хоти́те	хо́чет хотя́т

Exercises:

1. Read Dialogue 5.

2. Memorize several verbs you think will be the most useful to you.

3. Translate into Russian:

> You can go by bus.
> A museum will be in front of the post office.
> We want to send letters to Moscow.
> I need to get off at the second stop.
> How much is the computer?

4. Memorize Dialogue 5.

УРÓК ШЕСТÓЙ

В рестора́не

Ивано́в:	До́брый ве́чер. Мы зака́зывали четы́ре ме́ста на фами́лию Орло́в.
Официа́нт:	До́брый ве́чер. Пожа́луйста, пройди́те за мной. Вас устро́ит э́тот сто́лик?
Ивано́в:	Извини́те, но э́то сли́шком бли́зко к орке́стру. Я люблю́ му́зыку, но она́ не даст нам разгова́ривать.
Официа́нт:	Ну а э́тот ти́хий у́гол вам нра́вится?
Ивано́в:	Да, спаси́бо.
Официа́нт:	Что вы бу́дете пить?
Орло́ва:	Я возьму́ немно́го коньяка́.
Ивано́ва:	Я то́же.
Орло́в:	Господи́н Ивано́в, хоти́те попро́бовать ру́сский напи́ток? Я возьму́ "Столи́чную" (э́то сорт во́дки).
Ивано́в:	Коне́чно, с удово́льствием.
Официа́нт:	Вот меню́. Пока́ вы бу́дете его́ чита́ть, я принесу́ ва́ши напи́тки.
Орло́ва:	Спаси́бо. Господа́ Ивано́вы, дава́йте не бу́дем так официа́льно. Зови́те нас про́сто по и́мени: Татья́на и Серге́й. Вы́пьем за э́то.
Ивано́ва:	Коне́чно. С друзья́ми так бу́дет прия́тнее. За ва́ше здоро́вье!
Официа́нт:	Вы гото́вы зака́зывать?
Ивано́ва:	Да, я возьму́ голубцы́.

Орло́ва:	А мне пельме́ни.
Ивано́в:	Мне котле́ту (ку́рицу) по-ки́евски.
Орло́в:	Я возьму́ котле́ты с со́усом.
Официа́нт:	Мо́жно вам посове́товать не́сколько изве́стных ру́сских вин к обе́ду? Вот сухо́е вино́. А э́то сла́дкое и лёгкое.
Ивано́в:	Мы возьмём "Цимля́нское".
Официа́нт:	Хорошо́. Сейча́с принесу́.

— — —

Принесли́ зака́з. О́бе па́ры начина́ют есть.

— — —

Орло́в:	Дово́льны вы свое́й пое́здкой?
Ивано́ва:	О́чень! Москва́ так измени́лась. Не́которые места́ мы совсе́м не узнаём.
Ивано́в:	Мы уви́дели мно́го краси́вых мест, когда́ гуля́ли. Мы не по́льзуемся маши́ной. Тру́дно найти́ стоя́нку, и мно́го движе́ния.
Орло́ва:	Вот почему́ мы по́льзуемся трамва́ем, авто́бусом и́ли метро́. Мы берём маши́ну, то́лько когда́ е́дем в выходны́е дни за́ город.
Официа́нт:	Как обе́д? Всё в поря́дке?
Ивано́в:	Всё бы́ло отли́чно.
Ивано́ва:	Я давно́ не про́бовала тако́й вку́сной еды́.
Официа́нт:	Принести́ вам десе́рт и́ли ко́фе?
Ивано́в:	Нет, спаси́бо, принеси́те счёт, пожа́луйста.

Официа́нт прино́сит счёт. Ивано́в пла́тит и добавля́ет чаевы́е.

LESSON SIX

In the Restaurant

Ivanov: Good evening. We have made reservations for four under the name of Orlov.

Waiter: Good evening. Please follow me. Would this table be all right for you?

Ivanov: I am sorry, but this is too close to the orchestra. I love music, but it will make it impossible for us to talk.

Waiter: Well, do you like this quiet corner?

Ivanov: Yes, thank you.

Waiter: What shall I bring you to drink?

Orlova: I will take a bit of cognac.

Ivanova: So will I.

Orlov: Mr. Ivanov, would you like to try a Russian drink? I will have "Stolichnaya"; this is a brand of vodka.

Ivanov: Of course, with pleasure.

Waiter: Here are your menus. While you read them I will bring your drinks.

Orlova: Thank you. Mr. and Mrs. Ivanov, let's not be so formal anymore. Call us simply by our first names: Tatiana and Sergei. Let's drink to that.

Ivanova: Of course! This way it's more pleasant between friends. Cheers! (Here is to your health.)

Waiter: Are you ready to order?

Ivanova: Yes. I'll have stuffed cabbage rolls.

Orlova: And I'll take "pelmeny" (a type of Russian ravioli).

Ivanov: I will have chicken "a la Kiev."

Orlov: I will take ground beef patties with sauce.

Waiter: May I suggest to you some well known Russian wines for
            your dinner? Here is a dry wine. And this one is sweet
            and light.

Ivanov: I'll take the "Tsimlyanskoye" (popular Russian wine).

Waiter: Very well. I'll bring it right away.

                    —   —   —

            The food is brought. Both couples begin to eat.

                    —   —   —

Orlov: Are you enjoying your visit here?

Ivanova: Very much! Moscow has changed so much. Some places
            we don't recognize at all.

Ivanov: We saw many beautiful places during our walks. We
            don't use the car. It is difficult to find a place to park,
            and the traffic is so heavy. (There is so much traffic)

Orlova: That's why we use the tram, the bus and the subway. We
            take the car only when we go to the country on weekends.

Waiter: How was your dinner? Was everything all right?

Ivanov: Everything was excellent.

Ivanova: It's been a long time since I've had such delicious food.

Waiter: Shall I bring you some dessert or coffee?

Ivanov: No, thank you; just bring the check, please.

The waiter brings the bill. Ivanov pays and adds the tip.

68

VOCABULARY

шестóй	sixth	прóсто	simply
четы́ре	four	по и́мени	by first name
мéсто	place	вы́пьем	let's drink
официáнт	waiter	с друзья́ми	with friends
за мной	after me	так	so
устрóить	to be all right	прия́тнее	more pleasant
э́тот	this	здорóвье	health
стóлик	table	готóвы	ready
извини́те	excuse me	голубцы́	stuffed cabbage rolls
бли́зко	close		
оркéстр	orchestra	пельмéни	"ravioli"
мýзыка	music	кýрица	chicken
не даст	will not let	по-ки́евски	a la Kiev
разговáривать	talk	котлéта	patty
ти́хий	quiet	сóус	sauce
ýгол	corner	мóжно	may
нрáвиться	like	посовéтовать	suggest
взять, возьмý	take/I'll take	нéсколько	a few/some
немнóго	some/a little	извéстных	well known
конья́к	cognac	винó	wine
я тóже	so do I	сухóе	dry
попрóбовать	try	слáдкое	sweet
рýсский	Russian	лёгкое	light
напи́ток	beverage	хорошó	good/well
сорт	brand	принесли́	brought
вóдка	vodka	закáз	order
конéчно	of course	начинáть	start
с удовóльст- вием	with pleasure	довóльны	satisfied
		своéй	your
меню́	menu	измени́лась	changed
покá	while	нéкоторые	some
читáть	read	совсéм	at all
принесý	I'll bring	узнáть	recognize
официáльно	official	уви́дели	saw
зови́те	call (command)	краси́вый	beautiful
		гуля́ли	walked

(гуля́ть)	(walk)	мой/моя́/моё	my (-,-,-)
по́льзоваться	use	мой	
тру́дно	hard	твой/твоя́/твоё/	your (-,-,-;
найти́	find	твой	singular,
движе́ние	traffic		familiar)
вот почему́	that's why	его́	his
брать, берём	take	её	her
выходны́е дни	days off	наш/на́ша/	our
за́ город	to the	на́ше/на́ши	
	countryside	ваш/ва́ша/ва́ше/	your
бы́ло	was/were	ва́ши	(-,-,- plural,
давно́	a long time		polite)
	since	ли	if (interroga-
не про́бовала	didn't try		tive)
тако́й	such/so	почему́	why
вку́сной	delicious	заче́м	what for
еда́	food	како́й/кака́я/	what kind
десе́рт	dessert	како́е/каки́е	
ко́фе	coffee	отку́да	where from
принеси́те	bring	понеде́льник	Monday
	(command)	вто́рник	Tuesday
приноси́ть	bring	среда́	Wednesday
счёт	bill	четве́рг	Thursday
плати́ть	pay	пя́тница	Friday
добавля́ть	add	суббо́та	Saturday
чаевы́е	tips	воскресе́нье	Sunday

Expressions:

Пройди́те за мной. - Follow me.
Что вы бу́дете пить? - What would you like to drink?
С удово́льствием. - With pleasure.
Коне́чно. - Of course.
Зови́те нас про́сто по и́мени. - Call us simply by our first names.
Вы́пьем за э́то. - Let's drink to that.
За ва́ше здоро́вье. - Cheers! (Here is to your health!)
Дово́льны ли вы свое́й пое́здкой? - Are you enjoying your visit here?
Всё бы́ло отли́чно. - Everything was excellent.

GRAMMAR

1. Possessive pronouns.
Like personal pronouns, the possessive pronouns (my, your, his, etc.)
also change according to the case as well as gender; there are also the
plural forms.

	masculine	feminine	neuter	plural
my	мой	моя́	моё	мои́
your(s)	твой	твоя́	твоё	твои́
our(s)	наш	на́ша	на́ше	на́ши
your(s) (pl.)	ваш	ва́ша	ва́ше	ва́ши

His, her, its, and their(s) have only one form for all genders and for
plural:
his - его́ (is pronounced as "evo"); her(s) - её; its - его́; their(s) - их.

The possessive pronouns agree with the noun to which they refer;
therefore "my wife" is моя́ жена́; my son - мой сын; my children -
мои́ де́ти.

2. Asking questions.

There are two ways to ask a question in Russian. One is to use an
intonation where the voice rises on the stressed syllable of the main
word of the question. The word order is not important as it is in
English.

Examples:

Do you know the address? - Вы зна́ете а́дрес?
Do you speak Russian? - Вы говори́те по-ру́сски?

The other way is to use a question word or the particle ли. The question word is usually placed at the beginning of the sentence and the particle **ли** - behind the main word of the question, provided there is no question word.

Examples:

Are you going to the hotel? - Идёте ли вы в гости́ницу?
Do you speak Russian? - Говори́те ли вы по-ру́сски?
Where is our hotel? - Где на́ша гости́ница?

3. Question words

who	кто	what for	заче́м
what	что	what kind	како́й/кака́я како́е/каки́е
where	где	when	когда́
why	почему́	where from	отку́да
where to	куда́	how	как

4. Days of the week:

Monday	понеде́льник
Tuesday	вто́рник
Wednesday	среда́
Thursday	четве́рг
Friday	пя́тница
Saturday	суббо́та
Sunday	воскресе́нье

Exercises:

1. Read Dialogue 6.

2. Memorize possessive pronouns and question words.

3. Translate into Russian and give your answers to these questions:

> Where do you (plural) live?
> Where is your hotel?
> When do you go (by transport) to Moscow?
> Do you speak Russian? (two ways)
> Do you like music? (two ways)
> What would you like to drink?
> Would you like to try vodka? (two ways)

4. Memorize Dialogue 6.

УРÓК СЕДЬМÓЙ

За покýпками

Иванóвы хотя́т пойти́ в знамени́тый магази́н ГУМ на Крáсной плóщади, а потóм за сувени́рами в магази́н "Берёзка".

Иванóва:	Быстрée, Николáй. Магази́н закрывáется в дéвять вéчера. Éсли мы опоздáем, то нáдо бýдет идти́ зáвтра в дéвять утрá.
Иванóва:	Дóбрый вéчер. Мы хоти́м купи́ть лéтний костю́м моемý мýжу.
Продавщи́ца:	Какóй вам нýжен размéр?
Иванóв:	Сóрок оди́н, сóрок два, я не увéрен.
Продавщи́ца:	У нас есть бéлые, бéжевые и голубы́е костю́мы вáшего размéра.
Иванóв:	А сéрые у вас есть?
Продавщи́ца:	Да, есть. Но они́, мóжет быть, бýдут вам малы́. Хоти́те примéрить? Примéрочная вот здесь.
Иванóв:	Спаси́бо. Как раз на меня́. Скóлько он стóит?
Продавщи́ца:	Семь ты́сяч рублéй.
Иванóв:	Так. Вот дéньги за костю́м.
Иванóва:	Скажи́те, пожáлуйста, где отдéл óбуви?
Продавщи́ца:	Вон там.
Продавщи́ца:	Что вам показáть?
Иванóва:	Я хочý бéлые тýфли на высóком каблукé. Размéр три́дцать вóсемь.
Продавщи́ца:	Вы мóжете найти́ сáмые рáзные фасóны здесь.

Ивано́ва: Я куплю́ вот э́ти.

Продавщи́ца: Извини́те, но сейча́с у нас нет э́того
                фасо́на три́дцать восьмо́го разме́ра.
                Мо́жет быть, полу́чим на сле́дующей
                неде́ле.

Ивано́ва: Спаси́бо. Я приду́ на сле́дующей неде́ле.

LESSON SEVEN

Shopping

The Ivanovs want to go to the famous GUM (State Department Store or Moscow Mall) on Red Square, and later to shop for souvenirs in the store called "Beriozka."

Ivanova: Hurry up, Nikolai. The store closes at 9 p.m. If we are late we'll have to go tomorrow at 9 a.m.

Ivanova: Good evening! I would like to buy a summer suit for my husband.

Saleslady: What size do you need?

Ivanov: 41 or 42, I am not sure.

Saleslady: In this size we have white, beige and light blue suits.

Ivanov: And do you have any gray ones?

Saleslady: Yes, we do; but they may be too small for you. Would you like to try one? The fitting room is right here.

Ivanov: Thank you. It fits me just right. How much does it cost?

Saleslady: 7,000 rubles.

Ivanov: Fine. Here is the money for the suit.

Ivanova: Could you tell me, please, where the shoe department is?

Saleslady: Over there. What would you like me to show you?

Ivanova: I'd like a pair of high heeled white shoes, size 38.

Saleslady:	You can find a great variety of shoe styles over there.
Ivanova:	I'll buy these.
Saleslady:	I am sorry, but right now we don't have this style in size 38. Maybe we'll receive them next week.
Ivanova:	Thank you. I'll come back next week.

VOCABULARY

седьмо́й	7th	бе́жевый	beige
за поку́пками	shopping	голубо́й	blue
пойти́	go	се́рый	gray
знамени́тый	famous	мо́жет быть	may be
ГУМ	GUM (Moscow Mall)	мал	too small
		приме́рить	try
		приме́рочная	fitting room
Кра́сная пло́щадь	Red Square	как раз	just right
сувени́р	souvenir	для меня́	for me
Берёзка	Beriozka (hard currency store)	ско́лько сто́ит	how much is it?
		семь ты́сяч	7,000
		де́ньги	money
быстре́е	faster/ hurry	отде́л о́буви	shoe department
закрыва́ться	close	показа́ть	show
де́вять	nine	ту́фли	shoes
е́сли ... то	if ... than	на каблуке́	heeled
опозда́ем	(we'll) be late	высо́кий	high
		три́дцать	30
на́до бу́дет	must	во́семь	eight
за́втра	tomorrow	са́мые ра́зные	a great veriety
до́брый ве́чер	good evening	фасо́н	style
ле́тний	summer (adjective)	куплю́ (купи́ть)	I'll buy
		полу́чим (получи́ть)	(we'll) receive
костю́м	suit	приду́ (приходи́ть)	(I'll) come
моему́ му́жу	for my husband		
продавщи́ца	saleslady	хоро́ший	good
ну́жен	need	но́вый	new
разме́р	size	большо́й	big/large
со́рок	40	дорого́й	expensive
со́рок оди́н	41	ма́ленький	small/little
со́рок два	42	ми́лый	nice
не уве́рен	not sure	краси́вый	beautiful
бе́лый	white	знако́мый	familiar

78

плохо́й	bad	э́тот, э́та, э́то,	this
дли́нный	long	э́ти	these
коро́ткий	short	тот, та, то,	that
прия́тный	pleasant	те	those

Extra words

оде́жда	clothing	проду́кты	groceries
фру́кты	fruit	о́вощи	vegetables
ю́бка	skirt	хлеб	bread
я́блоки	apples	блу́зка	blouse
молоко́	milk	виногра́д	grapes
брю́ки	pants	ма́сло	butter
бана́ны	bananas	руба́шка	shirt
сыр	cheese	апельси́ны	oranges
носки́	socks	колбаса́	sausage
клубни́ка	strawberries	колго́тки	pantyhose
я́йца	eggs	пе́рсики	peaches
пла́тье	dress	бу́лочка	bread roll
сли́вы	plums	пальто́	coat
пече́нье	cookies	анана́с	pineapple
сапоги́	boots	конфе́ты	candy
лимо́н	lemon		

Expressions:

Быстре́е! - Hurry!

Магази́н закрыва́ется в де́вять часо́в ве́чера. - The store closes at 9 p.m.

Како́й вам ну́жен разме́р? - What size do you need?

Я не уве́рен. - I am not sure.

Хоти́те приме́рить? - Do you want to try it?

Как раз на меня́. - It fits me just right.

Что вам показа́ть? - What would you like me to show you?

GRAMMAR

1. Russian adjectives.

Adjectives are also inflected. They agree with the noun in gender, number (singular or plural) and case. They can be recognized by these endings: masculine -**ый**, -**ий**, -ой; feminine -**ая**, -**яя**; neuter -ое, -ее. Plural for all genders is -**ые**, -**ие**.

Adjectives "big/large" and "small/little" (большо́й, ма́ленький) in all cases:

Cases	Masculine and neuter	Feminine	Plural
Nominative	большо́й маленьки́й	больша́я ма́ленькая	больши́е ма́ленькие
Accusative	with animated nouns = Gen.; with inanimated nouns = Nom.	большу́ю ма́ленькую	больши́х ма́леньких
Genitive	большо́го ма́ленького	большо́й ма́ленькой	больши́х ма́леньких
Dative	большо́му ма́ленькому	большо́й ма́ленькой	больши́м ма́леньким
Instrumental	больши́м ма́леньким	большо́й ма́ленькой	больши́ми ма́ленькими
Prepositional	большо́м ма́леньком	большо́й ма́ленькой	больши́х ма́леньких

Some other adjectives which are frequently used:

good	хоро́ший	beautiful	краси́вый
new	но́вый	bad	плохо́й
expensive	дорого́й	long	дли́нный
nice	ми́лый	short	коро́ткий
familiar	знако́мый	pleasant	прия́тный

2. Demonstrative pronouns "this" and "that".

	Masculine	Feminine	Neuter	Plural
This	э́тот	э́та	э́то	э́ти
That	тот	та	то	те

3. Patronymics are the forms of polite address to the people who are not on a first name basis. Patronymic means using the person's first name followed by his or her father's name with a special ending. For men add to the father's name ending **-ович, -евич**; for women add -**овна,** -евна.

Examples:

Ива́н Петро́вич, Илья́ Ива́нович, Васи́лий Влади́мирович, Никола́й Никола́евич.
Ири́на Петро́вна, Татья́на Льво́вна, Тама́ра Миха́йловна, Евге́ния Я́ковлевна.

Exercises:

1. Read Dialogue 7.

2. Recite back in Russian dialogues 1 & 2 from your English text of those dialogues.

3. Translate into Russian:

> Do you need a taxi? - Of course!
> Where would you like to go? - To the store for souvenirs.
> Here is the money for a suit.
> I want to buy these shoes.

4. Memorize Dialogue 7.

УРÓК ВОСЬМÓЙ

В гостя́х

Иванóва:	Орлóвы пригласи́ли нас на у́жин сегóдня вéчером.
Иванóв:	Как ми́ло. В котóром часу́?
Иванóва:	В семь часóв. Но ну́жно вы́ехать ра́ньше и купи́ть им пода́рки.
Иванóв:	Что ты хóчешь купи́ть?
Иванóва:	Цветы́, буты́лку вина́ и конфéты дéтям. Поторопи́сь, мы должны́ вы́ехать чéрез час.

Дóма у Орлóвых. Звонóк в дверь.

Орлóва:	Никола́й и А́нна здесь. Открóй, пожа́луйста.
Орлóв:	Дóбрый вéчер! Заходи́те! Тру́дно бы́ло найти́ наш дом?
Иванóв:	Нет, óчень легкó. Мы взя́ли такси́. Вот цветы́ хозя́йке и буты́лка вина́ для вас. А где же дéти?
Орлóва:	Они́ у ба́бушки. Каки́е краси́вые цветы́! Спаси́бо.
Орлóв:	Что вам предложи́ть, вóдку или конья́к?
Иванóва:	Я бу́ду конья́к.
Орлóв:	Я покажу́ вам кварти́ру. Она́ не óчень больша́я, но удóбная. Вот спа́льни и туалéты, а здесь, ря́дом с гости́ной, ку́хня.
Иванóв:	Чем-то очень вку́сно па́хнет. Что э́то?

Орло́ва:	Я пригото́вила традицио́нный ру́сский обе́д. Борщ, котле́ты, пиро́г с гриба́ми, селёдку, винегре́т и компо́т на десе́рт.
Ивано́ва:	Но, Татья́на, мы не мо́жем всё э́то съесть. Э́то мно́го да́же на неде́лю.
Орло́ва:	Посмо́трим.

По́сле у́жина.

Ивано́в:	Я сли́шком мно́го съел, но всё бы́ло так вку́сно. Спаси́бо.
Орло́ва:	Не́ за что. Пойдёмте в гости́ную.
Ивано́ва:	Я вам помогу́ убра́ть со стола́.
Орло́ва:	Нет, нет. Э́то мо́жет подожда́ть. Но шампа́нское не бу́дет ждать.

Че́рез два часа́.

Ивано́в:	Уже́ так по́здно. Пора́ нам идти́. Вы́зовите нам такси́, пожа́луйста.
Орло́в:	Коне́чно. (Берёт тру́бку.) До́брый ве́чер. Пришли́те, пожа́луйста, маши́ну по а́дресу: у́лица Го́голя, дом со́рок пять. Фами́лия - Орло́вы. Телефо́н - 489-12-63 (четы́ре-во́семь-де́вять, двена́дцать-шестьдеся́т три). Че́рез де́сять мину́т такси́ бу́дет здесь.
Ивано́ва:	Спаси́бо за прекра́сный ве́чер. Спаси́бо за гостеприи́мство. Татья́на, я вам за́втра позвоню́. Всего́ до́брого.
Орло́вы:	Всего́ до́брого. Сроко́йной но́чи.

LESSON EIGHT

Being a Guest

Ivanova: The Orlovs invited us to dinner tonight.

Ivanov: How nice! At what time?

Ivanova: At seven o'clock. But we have to leave earlier and buy them some gifts.

Ivanov: What do you want to buy?

Ivanova: Flowers, a bottle of wine and candy for the children. Hurry, we have to leave in an hour.

At the Orlov's home. The doorbell rings.

Orlova: Nikolai and Anna are here. Open the door please.

Orlov: Good evening! Come in! Was it difficult to find our house?

Ivanov: No, it was very easy. We took a taxi. Here are some flowers for the lady of the house and a bottle of wine for you. But where are the children?

Orlova: They are at grandma's. What beautiful flowers! Thank you.

Orlov: What can I offer you to drink; vodka or cognac?

Ivanova: I'll have some cognac.

Orlov: Let me show you our apartment. It's not very big, but comfortable. Here are the bedrooms and the bathrooms, and here, next to the living room, is the kitchen.

Ivanov: Something smells very delicious. What is it?

Orlova:	I prepared a traditional Russian meal (dinner): "Borshch," Russian ground beef patties, a mushroom pie, salt-herring, "vinaigrette" (cooked vegetable salad with beets) and compote for dessert.
Ivanova:	But Tatiana, we won't be able to eat all of this. It's too much even for a week.
Orlova:	We'll see.

After dinner.

Ivanov:	I ate too much; but everything was so delicious! Thank you.
Orlova:	You are welcome. (Don't mention it.) Let's go to the living room.
Ivanova:	I'll help you clear the table.
Orlova:	Oh, no. That can wait, but the champagne will not.

Two hours later.

Ivanov:	It's so late already. It's time for us to go. Do call a taxi for us, please.
Orlov:	Of course. (Picks up the receiver.) Good evening. Please send a taxicab to this address: Gogol Street, house 45 . The last name is Orlov and the telephone is 489-12-63 . Thank you. The taxi will be here in ten minutes.
Ivanova:	Thanks for a wonderful evening. Thanks for your hospitality. Tatiana, I will call you tomorrow.
Orlovs:	All the best. Good night!

86

VOCABULARY

восьмо́й	8th	пригото́вила	prepared (cooked)
пригласи́ли	invited		
сего́дня	today	традицио́нный	traditional
ве́чером	in the evening	обе́д	dinner
ми́ло	nicely	борщ	borshch (beet soup)
час	hour	пиро́г	pie/cake
вы́ехать	leave	с гриба́ми	with mushroom filling
ра́ньше	early		
им	them		
цветы́	flowers	селёдка	herring
буты́лка	bottle	винегре́т	Russian beet salad
де́тям	for children		
поторопи́сь	hurry	компо́т	compote
до́ма	at home	съесть	eat
у Орло́вых	at the Orlovs'	смо́жем	(we'll) be able
звоно́к	bell	всё	all, everything
дверь	door		
откро́й	open	да́же	even
заходи́те	come in	на неде́лю	for a week
тру́дно	difficult	посмо́трим	(we'll) see
бы́ло	was/were	съел	ate
о́чень	very	не́ за что	you are welcome
легко́	easy		
взя́ли (взять)	took	помогу́	(I'll) help
хозя́йка	hostess	убра́ть	clear
у ба́бушки	at grandma's	со стола́	from the table
предложи́ть	offer	подожда́ть	wait (a little)
покажу́	(I'll) show		
кварти́ра	apartment	ждать	wait
удо́бная	comfortable	шампа́нское	champagne
спа́льня	bedroom	по́здно	late
туале́т	bathroom	пора́	it's time to
гости́ная	living room	вы́зовите	call (command)
ку́хня	kitchen		
па́хнуть	smell	брать (берёт)	take

трубка	receiver	девятнадцать	19
пришлите	send (command)	двадцать	20
		тридцать	30
минута	minute	сорок	40
прекрасный	wonderful	пятьдесят	50
гостеприймство	hospitality	шестьдесят	60
позвоню	(I'll) call	семьдесят	70
один, одна, одно	1	восемьдесят	80
		девяносто	90
два, две	2	сто	100
три	3	двести	200
четыре	4	триста	300
пять	5	четыреста	400
шесть	6	пятьсот	500
семь	7	шестьсот	600
восемь	8	семьсот	700
девять	9	восемьсот	800
десять	10	девятсот	900
одиннадцать	11	тысяча	1,000
двенадцать	12	две тысячи	2,000
тринадцать	13	три тысячи	3,000
четырнадцать	14	четыре тысячи	4,000
пятнадцать	15	пять тысяч	5,000
шестнадцать	16	миллион	million
семнадцать	17	миллиард	billion
восемнадцать	18		

Expressions:

Откройте дверь. - Open the door.
Заходите. - Come in.
Это слишком много. - It's too much.
Посмотрим. - We'll see.
Я съел слишком много. - I ate too much.
Всё было так вкусно. - Everything was so delicious.
Это может подождать. - It can wait.
Не за что. - You are welcome.
Спасибо за гостеприймство. - Thank you for your hospitality.
Спокойной ночи! - Good night.

GRAMMAR

1. Plural of Russian nouns. The following are the forms of Russian nouns: masculine - стол (table), дом (house), врач (doctor); feminine - минýта (minute), недéля (week), дверь (door); neuter - письмó (letter), свидáние (meeting).

Nominative	столы́ домá врачи́	минýты недéли двéри	пи́сьма свидáния
Accusative	столы́ домá врачéй	минýты недéли двéри	пи́сьма свидáния
Genitive	столóв домóв врачéй	минýт недéль дверéй	пи́сем свидáний
Dative	столáм домáм врачáм	минýтам недéлям дверя́м	пи́сьмам свидáниям
Instrumental	столáми домáми врачáми	минýтами недéлями дверя́ми	пи́сьмами свидáниями
Prepositional	столáх домáх врачáх	минýтах недéлях дверя́х	пи́сьмах свидáниях

Foreign words like таксú (taxi), метрó (metro), пальтó (coat) are undeclinable (one form for all cases and plural).

2. Cardinal numerals.

Nouns agree with cardinal numerals as follows:
1 - оди́н рубль, однá минýта, однó письмó; agrees in gender with

the noun in nominative singular;

2 - (masculine and neuter) два рубля́, письма́, (feminine) две́ копе́йки; noun is declined in genitive singular;

3, 4 - четы́ре рубля́, письма́, копе́йки; noun is declined in genitive singular;

5 - пять, 6 - шесть, 7 - семь, 8 - во́семь, 9 - де́вять, 10 - де́сять, 11 - оди́ннадцать,

12 - двена́дцать, 13 - трина́дцать, 14 - четы́рнадцать, 15 - пятна́дцать, 16 - шестна́дцать, 17 - семна́дцать, 18 - восемна́дцать, 19 - девятна́дцать, 20 - два́дцать рубле́й, пи́сем, копе́ек; nouns are declined in genitive plural. All numbers after 5 have this form unless the last digit is a 1, 2, 3, or 4.

Exercises:

1. Read dialogue 8.

2. Memorize cardinal numbers.

3. Translate into Russian:

> Where can I have breakfast, dinner?
> Could you tell me where the restroom is?
> Bring us the dessert and the bill please.
> Ivanov ate too much.
> Everything was delicious, thank you. - You're welcome.

4. Say in Russian:

> 2 rubles, 15 kopeks, 150 rubles, 7 houses, 3 weeks, 24 rubles, 5,000 rubles.

5. Memorize dialogue 8.

УРО́К ДЕВЯ́ТЫЙ

Боле́знь

Ра́но у́тром в ко́мнате гости́ницы.

Ивано́в: Я не зна́ю, что со мной, но я пло́хо себя́ чу́вствую.

Ивано́ва: У тебя́ что-нибу́дь боли́т? Ты о́чень бле́дный. Где у тебя́ бо́ли?

Ивано́в: Желу́док боли́т, голова́ то́же боли́т и кру́жится.

Ивано́ва: Дава́й позвони́м портье́ и попро́сим присла́ть врача́.

Прихо́дит врач (до́ктор).

Врач: До́брое у́тро. Я до́ктор Волы́нский. В чём де́ло?

Ивано́ва: Муж ужа́сно себя́ чу́вствует.

Врач: Пожа́луйста, ся́дьте. Разде́ньтесь до по́яса. Посмо́трим, кака́я у вас температу́ра. Так, чуть вы́ше норма́льной - три́дцать семь и шесть (37,6°С). Давле́ние норма́льное. Где боли́т желу́док? Здесь? Покажи́те язы́к. У вас расстро́йство желу́дка. Что вы вчера́ е́ли?

Ивано́в: О́чень мно́го всего́. Я был в гостя́х.

Врач: Ви́дно, вы не привы́кли к ру́сской пи́ще. О́чень вку́сная, но тяжёлая для желу́дка. Вам ну́жно побы́ть два дня на дие́те. То́лько чай, гре́нки и варёная карто́шка. Послеза́втра всё бу́дет в поря́дке. До свида́ния.

Ивано́в: До свида́ния.

LESSON NINE

Illness.

Early morning in the hotel room.

Ivanov: I don't know what's wrong with me, but I feel awful.

Ivanova: Do you have some pains? You are very pale. Where does it hurt?

Ivanov: I have a stomach ache, headache and I feel dizzy.

Ivanova: Let's call the front desk clerk and ask to have a doctor sent.

The doctor arrives.

Doctor: Good morning. I am Doctor Volynsky. What is the problem?

Ivanova: My husband feels terrible.

Doctor: Please sit up. Take off your clothing down to the waist. Let's see what your temperature is. Well, it's slightly above normal, 37.6°C. Your blood pressure is normal. Where does your stomach hurt? Here? Let me see your tongue. You have indigestion. What did you eat yesterday?

Ivanov: A great deal of everything. We were out for dinner at a friend's house.

Doctor: It seems you are not used to Russian food. It's very delicious, but heavy on the stomach. You'll have to be on a special diet for two days. Only tea, toast and boiled potatoes. The day after tomorrow everything will be all right. Good-bye.

Ivanov: Good-bye.

VOCABULARY

девя́тый	9th	тяжёлая	heavy
боле́знь	illness	побы́ть	stay
ра́но	early	на дие́те	on a diet
что со мной	what's wrong with me	два дня	for two days
		чай	tea
пло́хо	bad	гре́нки	toast
чу́вствовать	feel	варёный	boiled
боли́т	hurts	карто́шка	potato
боль	pain	послеза́втра	day after tomorrow
желу́док	stomach		
кру́жится голова́	feel dizzy	ви́за	visa
		пу́говица	button
портье́	porter	у меня́	I have
попроси́ть	ask	у тебя́	you have
присла́ть	send	у него́	he has
приходи́ть	come	у неё	she has
в чём де́ло	what's the problem	у нас	we have
		у вас	you have
ужа́сно	terribly	у них	they have
ся́дьте	sit up	без	without
разде́ньтесь	undress (command)	о́коло	near
		для	for
до по́яса	to the waist	до	to/until
посмо́трим	let's look	от	from
чуть	a little	по́сле	after
вы́ше	higher	у	by/near
норма́льный	normal	к	to/toward
давле́ние	blood pressure	по	by
покажи́те	show (command)	в	in/into
		на	on/onto
язы́к	tongue	про	about
расстро́йство желу́дка	indigestion	че́рез	across/after/in
		за	behind/during/for
всего́	of everything		
в гостя́х	visit	пе́ред	before/in front
ви́дно	it seems	с	with
привыка́ть	used to	о	about/regarding
пи́ща	food, meal		

не	not	дире́ктор	director
понима́ть	understand	америка́нец	American
здесь нет	here is no	америка́нка	American woman
ещё	yet		
го́род	city		

Extra words:

лоб	forehead	спина́	back
нос	nose	се́рдце	heart
глаз(-а́)	eye(s)	лёгкие	lungs
лицо́	face	нога́	leg
рот	mouth	коле́но	knee
у́хо (у́ши)	ear (ears)	рука́	hand/arm
грудь	chest	па́лец	finger

Expressions:

Я пло́хо себя́ чу́вствую. - I feel bad.
У меня́ боли́т желу́док (живо́т), голова́. - I have a stomach ache, a headache.
У меня́ голова́ кру́жится. - I feel dizzy.
Температу́ра три́дцать семь и шесть. - Temperature is 37.6°C.
Температу́ра вы́ше норма́льной. - You have a fever.
В чём де́ло? - What is the problem?

Extra expressions:

У вас что-нибу́дь боли́т? - Does anything hurt?
У меня́ боли́т го́рло. - I have a sore throat.
У меня́ ка́шель. - I am coughing.
Я бере́менна. - I am pregnant.
Пришли́те врача́. - Call a doctor.

GRAMMAR:

1. The past tense of Russian verbs.

This is indeed the easiest part of Russian grammar, unless the verb is irregular. For most verbs, one must drop the infinitive (dictionary) ending -ть, -ти and for masculine add -л, for feminine -ла, for neuter -ло, and for plural -ли.

Examples:

to read - чита́ть	past tense: чита́л, чита́ла, чита́ли
to prepare - приготовить	past tense: приготовил, пригото́вила, пригото́вили;
to show - показа́ть	past tense: показа́л, показа́ла, показа́ли.
to go (irregular) - идти́	past tense: шёл, шла, шло, шли.
to drive/ride - éхать	past tense: éхал, éхала, éхало, éхали.

2. The expression "to have" in Russian.

Unlike English, Russian uses the genitive case of all the pronouns preceded by the preposition **у** to express the meaning "to have." To express possession, the verb "to be" (**есть**) in present tense is used.

I have	У меня́ (есть)	I have guests.	У меня́ го́сти.
You have	У тебя́ (есть)	You have a car.	У тебя́ (есть) маши́на.
He has	У него́ (есть)	He has our luggage.	У него́ (есть) наш бага́ж.
She has	У неё (есть)	She has a visa.	У неё есть ви́за.

It has	У него́ (есть)	It (coat) has buttons.	У него́ (пальто́) есть пу́говицы.
We have	У нас (есть)	We have children.	У нас (есть) де́ти.
You have (plural)	У вас (есть)	You have the gifts.	У тебя́ (есть) пода́рки.
They have	У них (есть)	They have an apartment.	У них есть кварти́ра.

3.   Most frequently used prepositions and their cases, i.e. cases that follow them.

Followed by the genitive case:

> Without - **без.**
> Near - **о́коло́.**
> For - **для.**
> Before, up to, until, as far as - до.
> From, away from, from ... to - от.
> After - **по́сле.**
> At, "to have", by, near - **у.**

Followed by the dative case:

> To, toward (motion), by the time - к(ко).
> Around, about, along, during - **по.**

Followed by the accusative case:

> To, into (direction) - в.
> On, to (direction), for (time) - **на.**
> About, concerning - **про.**
> Across, after, in (time) - **че́рез.**

Followed by the instrumental case:

> Behind, during - за.
> Before, in front of - пе́ред.
> With - с.

Followed by the prepositional case:

> In (location, place) - в.
> On, by - на.
> About, concerning - о.

4. Negatives (no, not)

To negate a verb use **не**. <u>Example</u>: I don't understand. - Я **не** понима́ю.

To negate a noun, either a person or place, or object also use **не**. <u>Examples</u>: It is not a director. - Э́то **не** дире́ктор. I am not an American (American woman). - Я **не** америка́нец (америка́нка). This is not America. - Э́то **не** Аме́рика.

To express the absence of anything, or to say "no" use **нет**. <u>Example</u>: There is no telephone here. - Здесь **нет** телефо́на.

Exercises:

1. Read dialog 9.

2. Make your own sentences with the expression "to have" in Russian.

3. Translate into Russian using correct cases with different prepositions:

> This store is near the museum.
> Do you live in Moscow?
> I buy flowers for Tatiana and candy for children.
> I read about Russia.

We are going along the street.
The restaurant is in front of the bar near the staircase.

4. Say these Russian phrases in the past tense:

Мы приглашáем Ивáновых в гóсти.
Сергéй читáет о компьютерах.
Онú éдут по улице.

5. Memorize dialog 9.

УРÓК ДЕСЯ́ТЫЙ

На ве́чере для бизнесме́нов.

Петрóвы устрáивают "коктéль-пáрти" и приглашáют Орлóвых.

Иванóв:	Господи́н Петрóв, позвóльте познакóмить вас с нáшими рýсскими друзья́ми: Орлóвы, Татья́на и Сергéй. А э́то господи́н Петрóв, главá рýсского отделéния нáшей фи́рмы.
Петрóв:	Прия́тно познакóмиться. Вы тóже занимáетесь би́знесом?
Орлóв:	Нет. Я врач. А вы давнó рабóтаете с Иванóвым?
Петрóв:	Нет, мы подписáли контрáкт тóлько два дня назáд и начнём рабóтать вмéсте чéрез мéсяц. К томý врéмени мы закóнчим всю подготóвку дéла.
Иванóв:	Мы собирáем компью́теры в США и пересылáем их в Росси́ю. А все прогрáммы пи́шут здесь.
Орлóв:	Я увéрен, что э́то прекрáсная идéя. И врéмя для э́того хорóшее, так как сейчáс нам всё э́то óчень нýжно. Желáю успéха.
Иванóва:	Ужé пóздно. Нам нýжно уходи́ть. Самолёт улетáет рáно ýтром, а мы ещё не упаковáлись.
Орлóва:	Нам тóже нýжно уходи́ть. Сергéю рáно на рабóту. Спаси́бо за приглашéние. Нам бы́ло óчень прия́тно у вас на вéчере.
Иванóв:	Бы́ло óчень прия́тно с вáми познакóмиться. Вот моя́ визи́тная кáрточка. Когдá вы опя́ть бýдете в США, позвони́те нам, не забывáйте нас.

Орло́в: Спаси́бо. У вас уже́ есть наш а́дрес и теле-
фо́н. Счастли́вого пути́. Всего́ до́брого.
Споко́йной но́чи.

LESSON TEN

Socializing

At the Businessmen's Party

The Petrovs give a cocktail party and invite the Orlovs.

Ivanov: Mr. Petrov, let me (allow me to) introduce you to our Russian friends - the Orlovs, Tatiana and Sergei. And this is Mr. Petrov; he is the head of the Russian division of our firm.

Petrov: Nice to meet you. Are you also engaged in business?

Orlov: No, I am a doctor. Have you been working with Mr. Ivanov for a long time?

Petrov: No, we signed the contract only two days ago and we'll start working together a month from now. By that time we will have completed all of the business preparations. (All the paperwork.)

Ivanov: We assemble the computers in the USA and ship them to Russia. And all the software is written here.

Orlov: I am sure it's an excellent idea. The timing for this is good, because we now have a great need for this. Good luck.

Ivanova: It is late. We should be leaving. The plane leaves early in the morning and we still haven't packed.

Orlova: We should also be leaving. Sergei has to be at work early. Thank you for the invitation. We really enjoyed your party.

Ivanov: It's so nice to have met you. Here is my business card. When you come to the USA again, call us, and don't forget us.

Orlov: Thank you. You already have our address and telephone number. Have a good trip. All the best to you. Good night.

102

VOCABULARY

деся́тый	10th	програ́мма	software
ве́чер	party, evening	писа́ть (пишу́)	write
		прекра́сный	excellent
бизнесме́н	businessman	иде́я	idea
устра́ивать	give/arrange	вре́мя	time
коктéль-па́рти	cocktail party	так как	since
		жела́ть	wish
позво́льте	let me	успе́х	success
познако́мить	introduce	уходи́ть	leave
друг	friend	улета́ть	fly away
друзья́	friends	упакова́ться	get packed
глава́	head	рабо́та	work
отделе́ние	division	приглаше́ние	invitation
фи́рма	firm	визи́тная	business
то́же	too	ка́рточка	card
занима́ться	involved, occupied	опя́ть	again
		не забыва́йте	don't forget
би́знес	business	нас	us
давно́	long time	а́дрес	address
подписа́ть	sign	счастли́вого	have a good
контра́кт	contract	пути́	trip
начнём	(we'll) start	оди́ннадцатый	11th
вме́сте	together	двена́дцатый	12th
ме́сяц	month	трина́дцатый	13th
к тому́ вре́мени	by that time	четы́рнадцатый	14th
		двадца́тый	20th
зако́нчим	(we'll) finish	два́дцать пе́рвый	21st
подгото́вка	preparation		
де́ло	work, business	по́лдень	noon
		час/часа́/часо́в	o'clock, time, hour
собира́ть	assemble		
пересыла́ть	send over		

Expressions:

Позво́льте познако́мить вас с ... - Let me introduce to you ...
Прия́тно познако́миться. - Nice meeting you.

Желáю успéха. - Good luck.

Он пи́шет прогрáммы для компью́теров. - He writes computer software.

Э́то прекрáсная идéя! - It's an excellent idea!

Ужé пóздно. - It is late.

Вот моя́ визи́тная кáрточка. - Here is my business card.

Не забывáйте нас. - Don't forget us.

Састли́вого пути́. - Have a good trip.

GRAMMAR

1.   Ordinal numbers.

First	пе́рвый	Eighth	восьмо́й
Second	второ́й	Ninth	девя́тый
Third	тре́тий	Tenth	деся́тый
Fourth	четвёртый	Eleventh	оди́ннадцатый
Fifth	пя́тый	Twelfth	двена́дцатый
Sixth	шесто́й	20th	двадца́тый
Seventh	седьмо́й	21st	два́дцать пе́р-вый

Ordinal numbers have the same endings as adjectives.

2.   Telling time.

To ask "What time is it?" use the expressions "Ско́лько вре́мени?," "Кото́рый час?"
"In the morning" is "утра́;" "Noon" is "по́лдень;" "In the afternoon" is "дня;" "In the evening" is "ве́чера;" and "At night" is "но́чи." All these forms are genitive singular.

Exact hours are:

1 o'clock	час	4 o'clock	четы́ре часа́
2 o'clock	два часа́	5 o'clock	пять часо́в
3 o'clock	три часа́	6 o'clock	шесть часо́в

and so on to 12		18 o'clock	восемна́дцать часо́в
12 o'clock	двена́дцать часо́в	24 o'clock	два́дцать четы́ре часа́

The easiest way to tell time is the same as in English: 8:15 or "eight fifteen" would be "во́семь пятна́дцать"; "six thirty" would be "шесть три́дцать".

However, Russians tell time in a more complicated way. After the exact hour time is told referring to the next hour. The first 30 minutes of each hour would be as follows:

8:15 would be "15 minutes towards the ninth hour" or "пятна́дцать мину́т девя́того"
6:23 would be "23 minutes towards the seventh hour" or "два́дцать мину́т седьмо́го"

The word "мину́та" is declined according to the rules for numbers. The hours are expressed by ordinal numbers in genitive singular.

The word "half an hour" is "полови́на." 6:30 is "полови́на седьмо́го."

The last 30 minutes of each hour would be as follows:

8:45 would be "9 o'clock without 15 minutes" or "без пятна́дцати мину́т де́вять"
6:53 would be "7 o'clock without 7 minutes" or "без семи́ мину́т семь"

The hours are expressed by cardinal numbers in the nominative case and minutes are expressed by cardinal numbers in the genitive case.

This is explained for your information if you should hear these forms.

106

3.　　　　Future tense.

The compound future tense uses the word "will/shall" ("to be" in the future tense, see grammar, lesson 5). <u>Examples</u>: "I will speak" is "Я бу́ду говори́ть"; "Will you drink?" is "Вы бу́дете пить?"; "We will have dinner" is "Мы бу́дем обе́дать." There is another way of forming the future tense, which brings us to the next point in grammar.

4.　　　　The aspects of Russian verbs: perfective and imperfective.

The Russian verb system, in addition to the three tenses (present, past, and future) also has the concept of two aspects: imperfective (the action of the verb in progress or process, repeated action, state of being or description); and perfective, which shows the same verb with some limitations (a beginning, completion, short duration, or one time action). Usually when you see a verb that you recognize but it has a prefix (usually по-, на-, про-, с-, у-), it is a perfective verb. Perfective verbs have no present tense; therefore, when you see a verb with a prefix it will be automatically the simple future, with the same endings as for the present tense of the imperfective verb. All this is mentioned not for memorization but for general information since most of the verbs in the dialogues are perfective (prefixed verbs). English does not have aspects but uses helping verbs, such as "began to," "stopped to," "said one time," etc. Aspects have many prefixes, but those mentioned above are the most common.

Exercises:

1. Read dialogue 10.

2. Make up your own dialogue "In the Hotel" and "Meeting People".

3. Say in Russian: 4 p.m., 11:15 a.m., 12 noon, 10:20 p.m., 5:45 a.m.

4. Say the following sentences in the future tense:

　　　　Он живёт в Москве́.

Вы еди́те десе́рт (о́вощи, котле́ты).
Я пишу́ письмо́.

5. Memorize dialogue 10.

KEY TO THE EXERCISES:

Lesson 1

2. Feminine, masculine, feminine, masculine, feminine, feminine.

3. Я врач.
   Моя жена - учительница.
   Это аэропорт.
   Спасибо, всё в порядке.
   Это моя жена.

Lesson 2

2. Здравствуйте. Доброе утро!
   Большое спасибо.
   До свидания.
   Желаю приятно провести время.

Lesson 3

3. Как дела? - Отлично.
   Давайте поедем домой.
   Вы знаете, где это?
   Остановитесь здесь, пожалуйста.
   Сколько с меня? Сдачи не надо.

4. Бабушку - genitive case; у выхода - genitive case; проверка - nominative case; в гостинице - prepositional case; чемодан - accusative case.

Lesson 4

2. Вы говорите по-русски?
   Я работаю в банке.
   Скажите, пожалуйста, где обмен валюты?
   Я говорю по-русски.

Lesson 5

3. Вы мо́жете е́хать на авто́бусе.
Музе́й бу́дет напро́тив по́чты.
Мы хоти́м посла́ть пи́сьма в Москву́.
Мне на́до сойти́ на второ́й остано́вке.
Ско́лько сто́ит компью́тер?

Lesson 6

3. Где вы живёте?
Где ва́ша/твоя́ гости́ница?
Когда́ вы е́дете в Москву́?
Вы говори́те по-ру́сски?/Говори́те ли вы по-ру́сски?
Вы лю́бите му́зыку?/Лю́бите ли вы му́зыку?
Что вы бу́дете пить?
Вы хоти́те попро́бовать во́дку?/Хоти́те ли вы попро́бовать во́дку?

Lesson 7

3. Вам на́до такси́? - Коне́чно!
Куда́ вы хоти́те идти́? - В магази́н за сувени́рами.
Вот де́ньги за костю́м.
Я хочу́ купи́ть э́ти ту́фли.

Lesson 8

3. Где я могу́ поза́втракать/пообе́дать?
Вы не ска́жете, где туале́т?
Принеси́те десе́рт и счёт, пожа́луйста.
Ивано́в съел сли́шком мно́го.
Всё бы́ло о́чень вку́сно, спаси́бо. - Не́ за что.

4. Два рубля́, пятна́дцать копе́ек, сто пятьдеся́т рубле́й, семь домо́в, три неде́ли, два́дцать четы́ре рубля́, пять ты́сяч рубле́й.

Lesson 9

3. Э́тот магази́н о́коло музе́я.
    Вы живёте в Москве́?
    Я покупа́ю цветы́ для Татья́ны и конфе́ты для дете́й.
    Я чита́ю о Росси́и.
    Мы идём по у́лице.
    Рестора́н напро́тив ба́ра о́коло ле́стницы.

4. Мы приглаша́ли Ивано́вых в го́сти.
    Серге́й чита́л о компью́терах.
    Они́ е́хали по у́лице.

Lesson 10

3. Четы́ре часа́ ве́чера, оди́ннадцать пятна́дцать утра́, по́лдень,
    де́сять два́дцать ве́чера, пять со́рок пять утра́.

4. Он бу́дет жить в Москве́.
    Вы бу́дете есть десе́рт (о́вощи, котле́ты)?
    Я бу́ду писа́ть письмо́.

Review Exercise:

Translate into Russian:

Where do you work?
We are tourists.
Do you have children?
This is a business trip.
What is your name? - My name is ...
Where is the luggage?
I don't speak Russian well.
What would you like to see?
Please call us.
We'll be here two weeks, years.
Thank you very much.
Here are some small gifts.
Everything is all right.
How are you?
Where do you live?
Please stop here.
How much is it?
How much is the dinner, the souvenir?
I have reserved a room, a seat (place), a table.
Where can I park the car?
What services do you have in the hotel?
Excuse me, could you tell me ...
Go straight; at the intersection turn right, left.
Use bus number 8, 12, 25.
You have to get off here.
I want to send letters by airmail.
Good bye.
Please follow me.
I will buy this suit.
Call me simply by the first name.
We use the subway or the bus.
Please bring the bill.
I would like (want) to buy souvenirs, shoes.
What would you like me to show you?
Do you want to try this?
I want to try on this coat, shoes, blouse.

They'll come back next week.
They invited us to dinner.
Show me, please.
We can not eat this.
We can not drink much.
Everything was delicious.
You are welcome.
Call the taxi, the porter, the clerk, the doctor.
I don't feel well.
What is the problem?
Who is the head of the office, the store?
Pleased to meet you.
We have signed the contract.
Soon we will start working together.
Our firm assembles computers.
This is an excellent idea.
Good luck!
Thank you for the invitation.
Here is my business card.
Have a good trip!

Extra expressions

I have a question. - У меня́ вопро́с.
Do you have time? - У вас есть вре́мя?
Did you have the flu? - У вас был грипп?
Write this, please. - Напиши́те э́то, пожа́луйста.
Speak slowly, please. I don't understand you. - Говори́те ме́дленно, пожа́луйста. Я вас не понима́ю.

VOCABULARY

а (1) - and/but
авиапо́чтой (5) - by airmail
а́дрес (10) - address
Аме́рика (1) - America
америка́нец (9) - American
америка́нка (9) - American woman
анана́с (7) - pineapple
анке́та (4) - forms
апельси́н (7) - orange
аэропо́рт (1) - airport
ба́бушка (1) - grandmother
бага́ж (2) - luggage
бана́ны (7) - bananas
банк (1) - bank
бар (4) - bar
бассе́йн (4) - swimming pool
бе́жевый (7) - beige
без (9) - without
бе́лый (7) - white
Берёзка (7) - Beriozka (hard currency store)
би́знес (10) - business
бизнесме́н (10) - businessman
бли́зко (6) - close

блу́зка (7) - blouse
боле́знь (9) - illness
боле́ть, боли́т (9) - hurt, hurts
боль (9) - pain

большо́й (5,7) - big/large
борщ (8) - borshch (beet soup)
боя́ться (1) - be afraid
брать (беру́) (6,8) - take
брю́ки (7) - pants
бу́дьте добры́ (2) - be so kind
бу́лочка (7) - bread roll
буты́лка (8) - bottle
быстре́е (7) - hurry
бы́ть (1) - to be
в чём де́ло (9) - what's the problem
в (1,9) - in/to
в гостя́х (9) - visiting
в ... раз (1) - for ... time
валю́та (4) - currency
варёный (9) - boiled
ваш, ва́ша, ва́ше, ва́ши (2,6) - your(s)
ве́чер (10) - party, evening
ве́чером (8) - in the evening
вещь (2) - thing
взве́сить (5) - weigh
взять, возьму́ (6,8) - take/I'll take
ви́дно (9) - it seems
визи́тная ка́рточка (10) - business card
ви́за (9) - visa
винегре́т (8) - Russian beet salad
вино́ (6) - wine
виногра́д (7) - grapes

114

вку́сный (6) - delicious
вме́сте (10) - together
во́дка (6) - vodka
возвраща́ться (1) - return
восемна́дцать (8) - 18 (eighteen)
восемьсо́т (8) - 800 (eight hundred)
во́семь (8) - 8 (eight)
во́семьдесят (8) - 80 (eighty)
воскресе́нье (6) - Sunday
восьмо́й (8) - 8th (eighth)
вот почему́ (6) - that's why
врач (1,9) - doctor
вре́мя (2,10) - time
всё (8) - all/everything
все (3) - everybody
всего́ (9) - of everything
встре́тить (3) - meet (perfective)
встре́ча (1) - meeting
встреча́ть (3) - meet (imperfective)
вся (1) - all/whole
вто́рник (6) - Tuesday
второ́й (2) - 2nd (second)
вы (4) - you (plural or polite)
вы́ехать (8) - leave
вы́зовите (8) - call (command)
вы́пьем (6) - let's drink
высо́кий (7) - high
вы́ход (3) - exit

выходно́й день (6) - day off
вы́ше (9) - higher
гастроно́м (5) - food store
где (2) - where
глаз, глаза́ (9) - eye, eyes
говори́ть (2,4) - speak/talk
голубо́й (7) - blue
голу́бцы (6) - stuffed cabbage rolls
го́род (9) - city
господи́н (4) - Mister (Mr.)
гостеприи́мство (8) - hospitality
гости́ная (8) - living room
гости́ница (2) - hotel
гото́в, гото́ва, гото́во, гото́вы (6) - ready
граждани́н, гра́ждане (1) - citizen, citizens
грани́ца (1) - border
гре́нки (9) - toast
гриб (8) - mushroom
грудь (9) - chest
ГУМ (7) - GUM (Moscow Mall)
да (3) - yes
дава́йте (1,3) - let's
давле́ние (9) - blood pressure
давно́ (6,10) - for a long time
да́же (8) - even
два, две - 2 (two)

двадца́тый (10) - 20th (twentieth)

два́дцать (5,8) - 20 (twenty)

два́дцать пе́рвый (10) - 21st (twenty first)

две ты́сячи (8) - 2,000 (two thousand)

двена́дцатый (10) - 12th (twelfth)

двена́дцать (8) - 12 (twelve)

дверь (8) - door

две́сти (4,8) - 200 (two hundred)

движе́ние (6) - traffic

де́вочка (3) - girl

девяно́сто (8) - 90 (ninety)

девятна́дцать (8) - 19 (nineteen)

девятсо́т (8) - 900 (nine hundred)

девя́тый (9) - 9th (ninth)

де́вять (8) - 9 (nine)

де́ло (10) - work, business

де́ло (3) - matter

делова́я (1) - business (adj.)

де́ньги (7) - money

десе́рт (6) - dessert

деся́тый (10) - 10th (tenth)

де́сять (4,8) - 10 (ten)

де́ти (1) - children

дире́ктор (9) - director

дли́нный (7) - long

для (2,9) - for

до (5,9) - to/untill

до по́яса (9) - the waist up

добавля́ть (6) - add

дово́лен, дово́льна, дово́льны (6) - satisfied

дое́хать (5) - reach (by transport)

до́лжен, -на́, -ны́ (3,5) - owe/must

дом (3) - house

до́ма (3,8) - at home

домо́й (3) - (to) home

дорого́й (7) - expensive

дочь (1) - daughter

друг, друзья́ (10) - friend, friends

ду́мать (3) - think

его́ (6) - his

его́ (2) - it, its

еда́ (6) - food

её (6) - her

е́здить (1) - drive/travel

е́сли (4,7) - if

есть (4) - there is/are

есть (5) - eat

е́хать (5) - drive/ride

ещё (9) - yet

ещё (4) - else

ждать (8) - wait

жела́ть (2,10) - wish

желу́док (9) - stomach

жена́ (1) - wife

же́нщина (1) - woman

жить (1,5) - live

за (9) - behind/during/for

за поку́пками (7) - shopping

за мной (6) - after me

за́ город (6) - to countryside
за́втра (7) - tomorrow
за́втрак (4) - breakfast
зака́з (6) - order (noun)
зака́зывать (4) - order (verb)
зако́нчить (10) - finish
закрыва́ться (7) - close
занима́ться (10) - involved, occupied
запо́лнить (4) - fill out
заходи́те (8) - come in (command)
заче́м (6) - what for
звоно́к (8) - bell
здесь (2) - here
здоро́вье (6) - health
здра́вствуйте (2) - Hello!
знако́мый (7) - familiar
знамени́тый (7) - famous
знать (3,5) - know
зови́те (6) - call (command)
и (1) - and
иде́я (10) - idea
иди́те (5) - go (command)
идти́ (5) - go (on foot)
из (1,4,9) - from
изве́стный (6) - well known
извини́те (6) - excuse me
измени́ться (6) - change
им (8) - them
и́мя (4) - name

их (3) - them/their
к тому́ вре́мени (10) - by that time
к (9) - to/toward
каблу́к, на каблуке́ (7) - heel, heeled
как (1) - as/like
как (5) - how
как до́лго (2) - how long
как раз (7) - just right
како́й/кака́я/како́е/ каки́е (6) - what kind
карто́шка (9) - potato
кварти́ра (8) - apartment
клубни́ка (7) - strawberries
ключ (4) - key
когда́ (4) - when
коктéль-па́рти (10) - cocktail party
колбаса́ (7) - sausage
колго́тки (7) - pantyhose
коле́но (9) - knee
ко́мната (4) - room
компо́т (8) - compote
компью́тер (1) - computer
коне́чно 2, (6) - of course/ sure/ certainly
конфе́ты (7) - candy
конья́к (6) - cognac
копе́йка (5) - kopecks
коро́ткий (7) - short
костю́м (7) - suit
котле́та (6) - patty
ко́фе (6) - coffee
краси́вый (6) - beautiful

Кра́сная пло́щадь (7) - Red Square
кра́сный (7) - red
кру́жится голова́ (9) - feel dizzy
кто (1) - who
куда́ (3) - (to) where
купи́ть (7) - buy (perfective)
ку́рица (6) - chicken
ку́хня (8) - kitchen
лёгкие (9) - lungs
лёгкий (6) - light
легко́ (8) - easy
ле́стница (4) - staircase
лет (год) (1) - years (year)
ле́тний (7) - summer (adj.)
ли (6) - if (interrogative)
лимо́н (7) - lemon
лифт (4) - elevator
лицо́ (9) - face
лоб (9) - forehead
люби́ть (5) - like/love
магази́н (4,7) - shop/store
мал (7) - too small
ма́ленький (7) - small/little
ма́ма (3) - mom
ма́сло (7) - butter
маши́на (3) - car
ме́лкий (2) - small
меню́ (6) - menu
ме́сто (6) - place
ме́сяц (1,10) - month
миллиа́рд (8) - billion
миллио́н (8) - million
ми́ло (8) - nicely

ми́лый (3,7) - nice
мину́та (8) - minute
мно́го (3) - much/many
мо́жет быть (7) - may be
мо́жно (6) - may
мой, моя́, моё, мои́ (1,6) - my (mine)
молоко́ (7) - milk
Москва́ (1) - Moscow
мо́чь (2,5) - can/may
музе́й (5) - museum
му́зыка (6) - music
мы (1,4) - we
на обе́д (3) - for dinner
на (4,9) - on/onto
на двои́х (4) - for two
на неде́лю (8) - for a week
на сле́дующей неде́ле (3) - next week
на дие́те (9) - on a diet
на́до (3,5) - need
наза́д (1) - ago
найти́ (6,8) - find
нале́во (5) - to the left
напи́ток (6) - beverage
напра́во (4) - to the right
напро́тив (4) - in front of
нас (1) - us
нача́ть, начнём (6,10) - start/begin, (we'll) start
наш, на́ша, на́ше, на́ши (2) - our
не (3,9) - not
не даст (6) - will not let

недалеко́ от (3) - not far
    from
неде́ля (2) - week
не́который (6) - some
немно́го (6) - some/a
    little
не́рвничать (1) - to be
    nervous
не́сколько (6) - a
    few/some
нет (1,9) - no
но (1) - but
но́вый (7) - new
нога́ (9) - leg
но́мер (4) - room
    number
норма́льный (9) -
    normal
нос (9) - nose
носки́ (7) - socks
нра́виться (6) - like
ну́жен, нужна́, ну́жно,
нужны́ (3) - need
ну́жно (4) - necessary
о (9) - about/regarding
о́ба, о́бе (1) - both
обе́д (8) - dinner
обме́н валю́ты (4) -
    currency
    exchange
о́вощи (7) - vegetables
оде́жда (7) - clothing
оди́н, одна́, одно́ (8) -
    1 (one)
оди́ннадцатый (10) -
    11th (eleventh)
оди́ннадцать (8) - 11
    (eleven)
о́коло (9) - near
око́шко (5) - window

он (4) - he
она́ (4) - she
они́ (4) - they
оно́ (4) - it
опозда́ть (7) - be late
опя́ть (10) - again
орке́стр (6) - orchestra
останови́ться (3) - stop
    (verb)
остано́виться (2) - stay
остано́вка (5) - stop
    (noun)
от (9) - from
отде́л о́буви (7) - shoe
    department
отделе́ние (10) -
    division
откро́й(-те) (8) - open
    (command)
откры́ть (2) - open
отку́да (6) - where from
отли́чно (3) - perfect
официа́льно (6) -
    official
о́чень (3) - very
па́лец (9) - finger
пальто́ (7) - coat
па́ра (1) - couple
парикма́херская (4) -
    hair salon
па́спорт (2) - passport
па́хнуть (8) - smell
пельме́ни (6) - "ravioli"
пе́рвый (1,10) - first
пе́ред (9) - before/in
    front
перекрёсток (5) -
    crossroads
пересе́чь (1) - cross

пересыла́ть (10) - send over

пе́рсик (7) - peach

пече́нье (7) - cookies

пиро́г (8) - pie/cake

писа́ть (10) - write

письмо́ (5) - letter

пить (5) - drink

пи́ща (9) - food/meal

плати́ть (6) - pay

пла́тье (7) - dress

пло́хо (9) - badly

плохо́й (7) - bad

по (9) - by

по и́мени (6) - by first name

по (1,9) - along, by

по-ки́евски (6) - a la Kiev

по-ру́сски (2) - in Russian

побыва́ть (10) - happen to be

побы́ть (9) - stay

поверни́те (5) - turn (command)

под (4) - under

пода́рок (2) - gift

подва́л (4) - basement

подгото́вка (10) - preparation

подожда́ть (8) - wait

подойди́те к (5) - come up to (command)

подойти́ к (5) - come up to

подписа́ть (10) - sign

пое́здка (1) - trip

поезжа́й (3) - go (command)

пое́хать (3) - go (by transport)

пожа́луйста (2) - please

поза́втракать (4) - have breakfast

позво́льте

познако́мить (10) - let me introduce

позвони́ть (8) - call

по́здно (8) - late

познако́миться (1) - get acquainted

пойти́ (7) - go

пока́ (6) - while

покажи́те (2,9) - show (command)

показа́ть (7) - show

покупа́ть (5) - buy

по́лдень (10) - noon

получа́ть (5) - receive

получи́ть (2,7) - receive/pick up

по́льзоваться (6) - use

помо́чь, помогу́ (8) - help, (I'll) help

понеде́льник (6) - Monday

понима́ть (9) - understand

пообе́дать (8) - have dinner/lunch

попро́бовать (6) - try

попроси́ть (4,9) - ask for

пора́ (8) - it's time to

портье́ (9) - porter

поса́дка (1) - landing

посла́ть (5) - send

по́сле (9) - after

послезáвтра (9) - day after tomorrow
посмотрéть (2) - to see
посмóтрим (9) - let's look
посмóтрим (8) - (we'll) see
посовéтовать (6) - suggest
постáвить (4) - place/put/park
посы́лки (5) - packages
поторопи́сь (8) - hurry (command)
поýжинать - have supper/dinner
почемý (1,6) - why
пóчта (4) - post office
прáвда (3) - true
предложи́ть (8) - offer
предъявлéние (2) - declaration
прекрáсный (8) - wonderful/ excellent
привыкáть (9) - used to
пригласи́ть (8) -invite (perfective)
приглашéние (10) - invitation
приглашáть (5) - invite (imperfective)
приготóвить (8) - prepare/cook
придý (7) - (I'll) come
приéзд (2) - arrival
приéхать (4) - arrive
приземля́ться (1) - land
примéрить (7) - try
примéрочная (7) - fitting room
принеси́те (6) - bring me (command)
принести́ (4) - bring (perfective)
приноси́ть (6) - bring (imperfective)
присла́ть (9) - send
приходи́ть (9) - come
пришли́те (8) - send (command)
прия́тнее (6) - more pleasant
прия́тно познакóмиться (10) - nice to meet you
прия́тно (2) - nicely/pleasantly
прия́тный (7) - pleasant
про (9) - about
прóбовать (6) - try
провéрка (2) - check
провести́ (2) - spend
продавáть (1) - sell
продýкты (7) - groceries
пройди́те (2) - go (command)
пройти́ (5) - go to
прости́те (1) - excuse me
прóсто (6) - simply
профéссия (1) - profession
пря́мо (5) - straight
пýговица (9) - button
путь (10) - way/trip
пятнáдцать (8) - 15 (fifteen)
пя́тница (6) - Friday
пя́тый (5) - 5th (fifth)

пять (8) - 5 (five)
пять тысяч (8) - 5,000 (five thousand)
пятьдесят (8) - 50 (fifty)
пятьсот (8) - 500 (five hundred)
работа (10) - work (noun)
работать (1,4) - work (verb)
разговаривать (6) - talk
разденьтесь (9) - undress (command)
размер (7) - size
разный (7) - various
рано (9) - early
раньше (8) - earlier
расстройство желудка (9) - indigestion
родиться (2) - to be born
родственник (1) - relative
российская (1) - Russian (of Russia)
Россия (1) - Russia
рот (9) - mouth
рубашка (7) - shirt
рубль (3) - ruble
рука (9) - hand/arm
русский (1,6) - Russian (nationality)
ряд (1) - row
рядом с (4,8) - next to
с (1,9) - with
с удовольствием (6) - with pleasure
с друзьями (6) - with friends
самолёт (1) - airplane
сапоги (7) - boots
светофор (5) - street light
свидание (3) - meeting
свой, своя, своё, свой (3) - used instead of any possessive pronoun
сдача (3) - change
сегодня (8) - today
седьмой (7) - 7th (seventh)
сейчас (1) - now
сейчас же (4) - just now
селёдка (8) - herring
семнадцать (8) - 17 (seventeen)
семь (8) - 7 (seven)
семьдесят (8) - 70 (seventy)
семьсот (8) - 700 (seven hundred)
сердце (9) - heart
серый (7) - gray
сидеть (1) - sit
скажите (4,7) - tell me
сказать (5) - say/tell
сколько (5) - how much
скоро (3) - soon
сладкий (6) - sweet
слева (5) - from the left
слива (7) - plum
слишком (3,6,8) - too
слышать (4) - hear
смотреть (1) - look
смотрите (1) - look (command)
сначала (5) - first

собира́ть (10) - assemble
совсе́м (6) - at all
сойти́ (5) - get off
со́рок (3,8) - 40 (forty)
сорт (6) - brand
со́ус (6) - sauce
спа́льня (8) - bedroom
спина́ (9) - back
среда́ (6) - Wednesday
сто (8) - 100 (one
    hundred)
сто́имость (4) - price
сто́ить (5) - cost
сто́лик (6) - table
стоя́нка (3) - stop/station
стоя́нка (4) - parking lot
страна́ (1) - country
суббо́та (6) - Saturday
сувени́р (7) - souvenir
сухо́й (6) - dry
счастли́вый (10) - happy
счёт (6) - bill
счётчик (3) - taximeter
США (1) - USA
съесть (8) - eat
сын (1) - son
сыр (7) - cheese
ся́дете (3) - (you'll) sit
ся́дьте (9) - sit up
    (command)
так (6) - so
так как (10) - since
тако́й (6) - such/so
такси́ (3) - taxi
там (1) - there
тамо́женник (2) -
    customs officer
тамо́жня (2) - customs
твой/твоя́/твоё/твои́ -
    your (singular,

    familiar)
тепе́рь (2) - now
ти́хий (6) - quiet
то́же (6,10) - too
то́лько что (1) - just
    now
то́лько (2) - only
тот, та, то, те (7) - that,
    those
традицио́нный (8) -
    traditional
тре́тий (3) - 3rd (third)
три ты́сячи (8) - 3,000
    (three thousand)
три (8) - 3 (three)
три́дцать (8) - 30
    (thirty)
трина́дцатый (10) -
    13th (thirteenth)
трина́дцать (8) - 13
    (thirteen)
три́ста (8) - 300 (three
    hundred)
тру́бка (8) - receiver
тру́дно (6,8) -
    difficult/hard
туале́т (8) - bathroom
туда́ (1) - (to) there
тури́ст (1) - tourist
ту́фли (7) - shoes
ты (4) - you (familiar)
ты́сяча (8) - 1,000 (one
    thousand)
тяжёлая (9) - heavy
у (9) - by/near
у них (9) - they have
у нас (9) - we have
у неё (9) - she has
у меня́ (9) - I have
у вас (1,9) - you have

у тебя́ (9) - you have
у ба́бушки (8) - at
    grandma's
у него́ (9) - he has
убра́ть (8) - clear
уве́рен, уве́рена,
    уве́рены (1) -
    sure/certain
уви́деть (1,3) - see
уви́димся (3) - we'll
    meet
у́гол (6) - corner
удо́бный (8) -
    comfortable
уе́хать (1) - left
ужа́сно (9) - terribly
уже́ (1,8) - already
узна́ть (6) - recognize
улета́ть (10) - fly away
у́лица (3) - street
у́личная про́бка (3) -
    street jams
упакова́ться (10) - get
    packed
уро́к (1) - lesson
услу́га (4) - service
успе́х (10) - success
устра́ивать (10) -
    give/arrange
устро́ить (6) - to be all
    right
утра́ (4) - in the morning
у́хо (у́ши) (9) - ear
    (ears)
уходи́ть (10) - leave
учи́тельница (1) -
    teacher
фами́лия (2) - last name
фасо́н (7) - style
фи́рма (10) - firm

фру́кты (7) - fruit
хлеб (7) - bread
ходи́ть (1) - go
хозя́йка (8) - hostess
хоро́ший (7) - good
хорошо́ (6) - good/well
хоте́ть (1,5) - want
цвето́к, цветы́ (8) -
    flower, flowers
центр го́рода (3) -
    downtown
чаевы́е (6) - tips
чай (9) - tea
час (часа́, часо́в) (10) -
    o'clock, time,
    hour
челове́к (3) - persons
чемода́н (2) - suitcase
че́рез (5,9) -
    across/after/in
четве́рг (6) - Thursday
четвёртый (4) - 4th
    (fourth)
четы́ре (8) - 4 (four)
четы́ре ты́сячи (8) -
    4,000 (four
    thousand)
четы́реста (3,8) - 400
    (four hundred)
четы́рнадцатый (10) -
    14th (fourteenth)
четы́рнадцать (8) - 14
    (fourteen)
чита́ть (6,9) - read
что (1,5) - that/what
что со мной (9) -
    what's wrong
    with me
что-нибу́дь (9) -
    anything/something

чтóбы (4) - to
чу́вствовать (9) -
    feel
чуть (9) - a little
шампа́нское (8) -
    champagne
шестна́дцать (8) - 16
    (sixteen)
шестóй (6) - 6th (sixth)
шесть (5,8) - 6 (six)
шестьдеся́т (8) - 60
    (sixty)
шестьсóт (5,8) - 600
    (six hundred)

шкóла (1) - school
шофёр (3) - driver
эмигри́ровать (1) -
    emigrate
эта́ж (4) - floor
э́тот, э́та, э́то, э́ти (7) -
    this, these
ю́бка (7) - skirt
я (1) - I
я́блоки (7) - apples
язы́к (9) - tongue
яйцó, я́йца (7) - egg,
    eggs

Russian-English Expressions:

Большо́е спаси́бо! - Thank you very much!

Бу́дьте добры́! - Be so kind (please)...

Быстре́е! - Hurry!

В чём де́ло? - What is the problem?

Ваш но́мер на второ́м этаже́. - Your room is on the 2nd floor.

Вот стоя́нка такси́. - Here is a taxi stand.

Вот моя́ визи́тная ка́рточка. - Here is my business card.

Вот, пожа́луйста. - Here you are.

Всё бы́ло отли́чно. - Everything was excellent.

Всё бы́ло так вку́сно. - Everything was so delicious.

Всё в поря́дке. - Everything is all right.

Всего́ хоро́шего. - All the best.

Вы говори́те по-ру́сски? - Do you speak Russian?

Вы мо́жете дое́хать на трамва́е (авто́бусе, тролле́йбусе, метро́). - You can go by tram (bus, trolley bus, metro).

Вы мо́жете получи́ть свой бага́ж здесь. - You may pick up your luggage here.

Вы зна́ете, где э́то? - Do you know, where it is?

Вы не ска́жете, как пройти́ ... ? - Could you tell me, how to get (go) ... ?

Вы́зовите нам (мне) такси́. - Call us a cab.

Вы́пьем за э́то. - Let's drink to that.

Где мо́жно поста́вить маши́ну? - Where can I park the car?

Дава́йте пое́дем домо́й. - Let's go home.

Дава́йте познако́мимся. - Let us introduce ourselves.

До свида́ния. - Good bye.

До́брое у́тро! - Good morning!

До́брый ве́чер! - Good evening!

До́брый день. - Good day.

Дово́льны ли вы свое́й пое́здкой? - Are you enjoying your trip?

Е́сли вам что-нибу́дь ну́жно, да́йте нам знать. - If you need something, let us know.

Жела́ю вам прия́тно провести́ вре́мя. - Have a nice time.

Желаю успеха. - Good luck.

За ваше здоровье. - Cheers! (Here is to your health!)

Заполните эти анкеты. - Fill out these forms.

Заходите. - Come in.

Здравствуйте! - Hello!

Зовите нас просто по имени. - Call us simply by our first names.

Идите прямо/налево/направо. - Go straight/left/right.

Извините. - Excuse me.

Как дела? - How are you?

Как долго вы будете здесь? - How long will you stay here?

Как обед? - How is the dinner?

Как раз на меня. - Just right for me.

Какой вам нужен размер? - What size do you need?

Конечно! - Of course!

Кто вы по профессии? - What are your professions?

Магазин закрывается в девять часов вечера. - The store closes at 9 p.m.

Меня зовут ... - My name is ...

Моё имя ... - My first name is ...

Моя фамилия ... - My last name is ...

Мы живём в Москве (Нью-Йорке). - We live in Moscow (New York).

Мы хотим увидеть всю страну. - We want to see the whole country.

Нам повезло. - We are lucky.

Не забывайте нас. - Don't forget us.

Не за что. - You are welcome.

Он пишет программы для компьютеров. - He writes computer software.

Остановитесь здесь, пожалуйста. - Stop here, please.

Откройте дверь, пожалуйста. - Open the door, please.

Отлично! - Perfect!

Поверните налево/направо. - Turn left/right.

Пожалуйста, пройдите... - Please, go to ...

Позвольте познакомить вас с ... - Let me introduce to you ...

Покажите, пожалуйста, ... - Show me, please...

Принесите счёт, пожалуйста. - Bring the bill, please.

Пришли́те врача́. - Call a doctor.

Прости́те. - Excuse me.

Посмо́трим. - We'll see.

Прия́тно познако́миться. - Nice meeting you.

Пройди́те за мной. - Follow me.

С вас ... - You owe me ...

С удово́льствием. - With pleasure.

Сда́чи не на́до. - Keep the change.

Скажи́те, пожа́луйста ... - Could you tell me, please ...

Ско́лько сто́ит? - How much is it?

Ско́лько с меня́? Ско́лько я вам до́лжен? - How much is it? How much do I owe you?

Спаси́бо. - Thank you.

Спаси́бо за гостеприи́мство. - Thank you for your hospitality.

Споко́йной но́чи! - Good night.

Счастли́вого пути́. - Have a good trip.

Температу́ра вы́ше норма́льной. - You have a fever.

Температу́ра три́дцать семь и шесть. - Temperature is 37.6°C.

У вас есть де́ти? - Do you have children?

У вас что-нибу́дь боли́т? - Does anything hurt?

У меня́ ка́шель. - I am coughing.

У меня́ боли́т го́рло. - I have a sore throat.

У меня́ боли́т живо́т, голова́. - I have a stomach ache, a headache.

У меня́ голова́ кру́жится. - I feel dizzy.

Уже́ по́здно. - It's late.

Хоти́те приме́рить? - Do you want to try it on?

Чем вы занима́етесь? - What is your occupation?

Что вам показа́ть? - What would you like me to show you?

Что вы бу́дете пить? - What would you like to drink?

Э́то мо́жет подожда́ть. - It can wait.

Э́то прекра́сная иде́я! - It's an excellent idea!

Э́то сли́шком мно́го. - It's too much.

Я вам позвоню́. - I'll give you a call.

Я не уве́рен. - I am not sure.

Я съел сли́шком мно́го. - I ate too much.

Я пло́хо себя́ чу́вствую. - I feel bad.

Я бере́менна. - I am pregnant.

Here is a taxi stand. - Вот стоянка такси.

How are you? - Как дела?

How long will you stay here? - Как долго вы будете здесь?

How is the dinner? - Как обед?

How much is it? - Сколько стоит?

How much is it? How much do I owe you? - Сколько с меня? Сколько я вам должен?

Hurry! - Быстрее!

I heard (in masculine and feminine forms) that... - Я слышал (слышала), что ...

I am pregnant. - Я беременна.

I ate too much. - Я съел слишком много.

I am not sure. - Я не уверен.

I feel bad. - Я плохо себя чувствую.

I have a sore throat. - У меня болит горло.

I am coughing. - У меня кашель.

I have a stomach ache, a headache. - У меня болит живот, голова.

I feel dizzy. - У меня голова кружится.

I'll give you a call. - Я вам позвоню.

If you need something, let us know. - Если вам что-нибудь нужно, дайте нам знать.

It can wait. - Это может подождать.

It's late. - Уже поздно.

It's an excellent idea! - Это прекрасная идея.

It's too much. - Это слишком много.

Just right for me. - Как раз на меня.

Keep the change. - Сдачи не надо.

Let me introduce to you ... - Позвольте познакомить вас с ...

Let us introduce ourselves. - Давайте познакомимся.

Let's go home. - Давайте поедем домой.

Let's drink to that. - Выпьем за это.

My last name is ... - Моя фамилия ...

My name is ... - Моё имя ...

My name is ... - Меня зовут ...

Nice meeting you. - Приятно познакомиться.

Of course! - Конечно!

Open the door, please. - Откройте дверь, пожалуйста.

Please, go to ... - Пожа́луйста, пройди́те...
Show me, please... - Покажи́те, пожа́луйста, ...
Temperature is 37.6°C. - Температу́ра три́дцать семь и шесть.
Thank you very much! - Большо́е спаси́бо!
Thank you for your hospitality. - Спаси́бо за гостеприи́мство.
The store closes at 9 p.m. - Магази́н закрыва́ется в девя́ть часо́в ве́чера.
We are lucky. - Нам повезло́.
We want to see the whole country. - Мы хоти́м уви́деть всю страну́.
We'll see. - Посмо́трим.
What is your occupation? - Чем вы занима́етесь?
What would you like me to show you? - Что вам показа́ть?
What would you like to drink? - Что вы бу́дете пить?
What is the problem? - В чём де́ло?
What are your professions? - Кто вы по профе́ссии?
What size do you need? - Како́й вам ну́жен разме́р?
Where can I park the car? - Где мо́жно поста́вить маши́ну?
With pleasure. - С удово́льствием.
You are welcome. - Не́ за что.
You may pick up your luggage here. - Вы мо́жете получи́ть свой бага́ж здесь.
You can go by tram (bus, trolley bus, metro). - Вы мо́жете дое́хать на трамва́е (авто́бусе, тролле́йбусе, метро́).
You have a fever. - Температу́ра вы́ше норма́льной.
You owe me ... - С вас ...
Your room is on the 2nd floor. - Ваш но́мер на второ́м этаже́.

Self-Taught Audio Language Course

Hippocrene Books is pleased to recommend Audio-Forum self-taught language courses. They match up very closely with the languages offered in Hippocrene dictionaries and offer a flexible, economical and thorough program of language learning.

Audio-Forum audio-cassette/book courses, recorded by native speakers, offer the convenience of a private tutor, enabling the learner to progress at his or her own pace. They are also ideal for brushing up on language skills that may not have been used in years. In as little as 25 minutes a day — even while driving, exercising, or doing something else — it's possible to develop a spoken fluency.

Ukrainian Self-Taught Language Course

Everyday Ukrainian (Beginning Course)
10 cassettes (10 hr.), 342-p. text, $195.
Order #HUK10.

All Audio-Forum courses are fully guaranteed and may be returned within 30 days for a full refund if you're not completely satisfied.

You may order directly from Audio-Forum by calling toll-free 1-800-243-1234.

For a complete course description and catalog of 264 courses in 91 languages, contact Audio-Forum, Dept. SE5, 96 Broad St., Guilford, CT 06437. Toll-free phone 1-800-243-1234. Fax 203-453-9774.

EASTERN AND CENTRAL EUROPEAN
TRAVEL GUIDES FROM HIPPOCRENE

TALLIN
A traveler's guide to this medieval city of Estonia includes a fold-out map.
137 pages, color photos, maps, plans $9.95hb 0-87052-917-X

HUNGARY, INSIDER'S GUIDE
From Budapest to the Great Plain to following the Danube, this is a well-rounded and intriguing introduction.
366 pages, appendices, b/w photos, maps $14.95pb 0-87052-976-5

HUNGARY, A COMPLETE GUIDE
350 pages, color & b/w photos, maps $16.95hb 0-87052-368-6

POLAND, COMPANION GUIDE (Revised Edition)
"Hands down, this is the best guidebook to Poland in recent memory....Delightfully written."—*Samatian Review*
220 pages, b/w photos, maps $14.95pb 0-7818-0077-3

POLAND, INSIDER'S GUIDE
"Following his tips the tourist has the means of creating a unique travel experience."—*Booklist*
250 pages, b/w photos, maps $9.95pb 0-87052-880-7

POLAND'S JEWISH HERITAGE
Details nearly 250 places in Poland tracing the Jewish past, with a chronology dating back to the 13th century.
250 pages, maps, b/w photos, illustrations $16.95pb 0-87052-991-9

ROMANIA, COMPANION GUIDE
This guide offers comprehensive historical, topographical, and cultural views.
220 pages, maps $14.95pb 0-87052-634-0

RUSSIA, LANGUAGE AND TRAVEL GUIDE
Allow Russian natives to introduce you to the system and country they know so well, covering the best of food, sightseeing, and transportation.
250 pages, map, b/w photos $14.95pb 0-7818-0047-1

UKRAINE, LANGUAGE AND TRAVEL GUIDE
Written jointly by a native Ukrainian and an American journalist, this guide details the culture, the people, and the highlights of the Ukrainian experience, with a convenient (romanized) guide to the essentials of the Ukrainian language.
266 pages, maps, b/w photos $14.95pb 0-7818-0190-7

LANGUAGE AND TRAVEL GUIDES
FROM HIPPOCRENE

LANGUAGE AND TRAVEL GUIDE TO AUSTRALIA, by Helen Jonsen
Travel with or without your family through the land of "OZ" on your own terms; this guide describes climates, seasons, different cities, coasts, countrysides, rainforests, and the Outback with a special consideration to culture and language.
250 pages • $14.95 • 0-7818-0166-4

LANGUAGE AND TRAVEL GUIDE TO FRANCE, by Elaine Klein
Specifically tailored to the language and travel needs of Americans visiting France, this book also serves as an introduction to the culture. Learn the etiquette of ordering in a restaurant, going through customs, and asking for directions.
320 pages • $14.95 • 0-7818-0080-3

LANGUAGE AND TRAVEL GUIDE TO MEXICO, by Ila Warner
Explaining exactly what to expect of hotels, transportation, shopping, and food, this guide provides the essential Spanish phrases, as well as describing appropriate gestures, and offering cultural comments.
224 pages • $14.95 • 0-87052-622-7

LANGUAGE AND TRAVEL GUIDE TO RUSSIA, by Victorya Andreyeva and Margarita Zubkus
Allow Russian natives to introduce you to the system they know so well. You'll be properly advised on such topics as food, transportation, the infamous Russian bath house, socializing, and sightseeing. Then, use the guide's handy language sections to be both independent and knowledgeable.
250 pages • $14.95 • 0-7818-0047-1

LANGUAGE AND TRAVEL GUIDE TO UKRAINE, by Linda Hodges and George Chumak
Written jointly by a native Ukrainian and an American journalist, this guide details the culture, the people, and the highlights of the Ukrainian experience, with a convenient (romanized) guide to the essentials of the Ukrainian language.
266 pages • $14.95 • 0-7818-0135-4

(Prices subject to change.)

TO PURCHASE HIPPOCRENE BOOKS contact your local bookstore or write to: HIPPOCRENE BOOKS, 171 Madison Avenue, New York, NY 10016. Please enclose check or money order, adding $4.00 shipping (UPS) for the first book and .50 for each additional book.